PRAXIS AND PRAISE

To the memory of
Mount Oliver Institute, Dundalk,
1969-1992

Ithaca gave the journey
(Kavafis)

Eamonn Bredin

Praxis and Praise

A SENSE OF DIRECTION IN LITURGY

the columba press

First published in 1994 by
тhe columba press
93 The Rise, Mount Merrion, Blackrock, Co Dublin

Cover by Bill Bolger
Origination by The Columba Press
Printed in Ireland by
Colour Books Ltd, Dublin

ISBN 1 85607 114 6

Contents

Preface

The thirtieth anniversary of the promulgation of *The Constitution on the Sacred Liturgy* (4 December 1963) seemed an appropriate time to bring together some reflections on liturgical renewal. The first part of this book seeks to assess the achievements and shortcomings of liturgical renewal during those thirty years. Chapters one and two were written as reviews of the impact of that reform after fifteen years. Chapters three and four continue that process of review, acknowledging other issues which have emerged more clearly after twenty-five and thirty years respectively.

These chapters are followed by an *Interlude* which tries to identify the most fundamental problems facing our praxis and praise. It also introduces the chapters of the second part of the book, which attempt to address certain aspects of those problems.

This book makes no claim to give anything like an exhaustive account of the developing liturgical situation, or a comprehensive outline of future developments. Its concern, as the subtitle implies, is with a sense of direction, so the approach will be impressionistic and self-consciously incomplete.

Throughout the book I refer to 'liturgy', but I must confess that, generally, it is the eucharistic celebration that I have in mind.

Eamonn Bredin
September 1994

Part I

CHAPTER 1

The Liturgy:
Problems and prospects [1]

The trick is not to arrange a festivity.
The trick is to find people who can enjoy it.
(Nietzsche)

On 4 December 1963, at the end of its second session, the Second Vatican Council promulgated the *Constitution on the Sacred Liturgy*. Since then we have been living through the most profound, the most intensive and the most rapid liturgical changes our church has ever known. It would be tedious and unnecessary to try to enumerate even the most major changes that have taken place. It is enough to say that what is taken for granted today would have been unimaginable to many before the Council. But Vatican II did not simply institute a programme for the renewal of the church's rites, it also asked us constantly to take stock of our achievements even as we live them so that we might shape the future more critically and more imaginatively. However we would need greater distance in time and a longer period of stability in order to gain perspective – stocktaking or projection at this stage are necessarily myopic – although some things are coming into focus already.

For many people 'change' in the church has become synonymous with the renewal of the liturgy – it is at the Sunday eucharist that 'aggiornamento' becomes palpable. In attempting to revitalise its worship, the church was touching what is deepest in our lives. Yet despite the initial heart-searching or worry which may have accompanied the introduction of this renewal, both people and priests have shown great adaptability and have taken these changes in their stride. Dreams have been fulfilled and many people are delighted with all that has happened and are openly enthusiastic about worship today. The liturgy, however, was reformed not just for the sake of novelty or to exchange new rubrics for old but so that 'all the faithful be led to

that full, conscious and active participation in liturgical celebrations which is demanded by the very nature of the liturgy, and is
their right and duty by reason of their baptism ... and is the primary and indispensable source from which they are to derive the
true Christian spirit' (SC 14). 'The purpose of the sacraments',
the *Constitution* said, 'is to sanctify men, to build up the Body of
Christ, and finally to give worship to God' (SC 59). We would
naturally expect, then, that a massive programme of reform and
renewal with these objectives should bring about a radical and
profound revitalisation of Christian life. If the test of the liturgy
is the life of the people who celebrate it, we would expect renewal
in liturgy to effect renewal in life or at least create a vibrantly
new appreciation of the role of liturgy in life. But have our expectations been fulfilled?

A twofold problem
Those who have processed and commented on the data about
Catholic worship emerging from many different countries, maintain that this correlation between life and liturgy has not always
been achieved and that the new liturgy seems to have left the
inner core of many people's lives untouched. They point to a
twofold problem found almost everywhere: (a) that a sharp decline is evident in the number of those taking part in the renewed liturgy (40% drop in France in 4 years); (b) that some of
those who still 'frequent' the sacraments do just that and seem
unaware of the Christian implications of celebrating the sacraments. These problems were aired at recent synods, national
episcopal conferences have given them top priority in pastoral
programmes, and they have been the subject matter of many
bishops' pastorals. But the decline in interest and participation
continues and, while this is not confined to any age or class, it
causes most pain when it involves the young, the parents of the
future, the socially committed. These very fine people are saying
'no' to the church and a very loud 'no' to even its updated liturgy
and yet some of them retain a passionate belief in Jesus Christ
and his gospel. The old scapegoats of materialism, consumerism
and secularisation may go some way towards explaining this
phenomenon, but they do not explain the really new and disturbing pattern here: why do people who are trying to take the
gospel seriously also say 'I take no delight in your solemn assemblies' (Amos 5:21)?

Despite the progress in the whole area of worship since Vatican II, deep concern is being expressed about the effectiveness of sacramental celebration. The reasons are obvious – the sacraments make the church. This concern issues as a powerful call for conversion and commitment, for transformation in heart and life. But what can be done, priests ask, when all the people want is to 'hear Mass', to 'soak in' grace simply by 'being there', when they treat the sacraments in an automatic, quasi-magical way? On the other hand, priests are told that they should be demanding an interiorisation of what is being expressed sacramentally; that they must point out, as St Paul did, that it is sacrilege to attempt to share the Body of Christ in the eucharist when you ignore Christ as incarnated in those you meet or avoid in daily life; that people must be told to leave their gift at the altar and first be reconciled to their brother and sister and that that reconciliation will not happen just because they mumble their way through the penitential rite at Mass.

The Irish situation

At the level of statistics at least, the findings of the survey on 'Religious Practices, Attitudes and Beliefs in Ireland' (1974) seem to point to a situation that contrasts sharply with anything noted so far. Our 91% weekly Mass attendance is described there as 'exceptional, if not unique ... and ... represents a pastoral situation that can have few parallels in the contemporary world.' But lest we become complacent in our euphoria, it modestly added: 'It is a healthy base on which to develop and the opportunities for development are there.' The reference to 'opportunities' no doubt hints at what is revealed in the darker side of that report, disturbing figures which some people have taken as indicating the beginnings of a decline comparable to that experienced in other countries.

A *Furrow* article (October 1978), by M. P. Gallagher, drew attention to these less widely publicised but alarming figures (especially those for non-communicants), in a very striking way. 'A full church could be the opium of the clergy,' he said; 'The overall figure of 91% ... is the truth but not the whole truth'. He rightly, of course, insisted that we must listen to the double message of the report and do justice to the two sides. Nevertheless, if the statistics available for church-going could be taken as a true index of the state of Catholic faith in this country, there would

still be cause for great rejoicing. Cahal Daly, however, has
warned against indulging in complacency because of these figures: 'We know only too well the difference between religious
practice and religious commitment.' And he noted 'the early
warning signs over certain sectors of the population and culture'.
(*Doctrine and Life*, March-April, 1977)

In their Pastoral, *The Work of Justice*, the bishops pointed out that
'a high percentage of worshipping or practising Catholics does
not, of itself, make a society Christian; people can be 'Sunday
Christians' only, isolating their worship from their weekday
lives. One of the urgent needs in the church today is to remove
the partitions separating religion from life and tending to keep
religion confined to Sundays and to churches.' And they quote
with approval the prophets' scathing judgement on the religion
and worship of their contemporaries as 'a fake and a fraud ...
unless it is accompanied by respect for the rights of men and
especially of the poor'. The statement issued by the National
Conference of Priests in May 1978, declared that 'the main danger
to religion in Ireland is not unbelief but shallow belief, a convention retained but only on the margins of life, a religion without
challenge and without depth'. Yet it was very hopeful: 'Ireland
has every chance of remaining an exceptionally religious country ... what is needed is a new pastoral creativity among the
priests'.

A special problem
The quotations could be multiplied but the message is clear:
'churchgoing' or 'attendance' or 'conformity' is one thing, the
correlation between liturgy and the transformation of daily life
is a distinct but related question. Though a fall-off is taking place
among significant sub-groups, Ireland, unlike most other countries, is not yet experiencing a general decline in church attendance. Yet the second aspect of the twofold global problem, that
concerned with unmeasurables like on-going conversion, personal conviction and commitment, is obviously causing serious
anxiety here. And it cannot simply be confined to the urban centres because, as priests know, at any given parish Mass you will
find people for whom the whole thing seems to be a pointless
exercise, 'a weekly ordeal' as someone described it to me lately.
Some people who attend our Sunday assemblies come because
they would feel guilty if they stayed away. It may be that fear of

hell rather than love of God is the real incentive; they may see the eucharist not as an occasion for freely 'giving thanks' but as an obligation to be rather grudgingly fulfilled. Others are present because their absence would grieve parents, wife, child or neighbour.

At the practical level of actual celebration, this can cause great difficulty. Even a dedicated congregation finds it difficult to achieve wholehearted involvement at the best of times, but this becomes virtually impossible if it is trying to carry a group of uninterested people as well. This is not a totally new situation – the 'etchings' on church seating tell their own story of boredom and indifference ('Maguire knelt behind a pillar where he could spit/without being seen …') – and so, to speak of a 'weakening of faith today' with a note of nostalgia in the voice can be misleading. For many reasons we are now more aware of these problems and we must admit that they have risen to near crisis level. It is vitally necessary, then, to examine what is new in the situation and be willing to pay the price of discovering worthwhile solutions, no matter what they cost. This would involve studying the pattern in other countries, learning from what has already happened there, trying to isolate the difficulties in their experience that are akin to our own, so as to face up to them before it is too late. Above all it would mean being attuned to what is unique in the Irish situation and trying to read 'the signs of the times' by listening to those who feel driven to the fringes of our assemblies. We might then begin to tackle these problems in a realistic and creative way. Listening is indispensable, listening to the complaints and criticisms of sincere and dedicated people, all of whom desire to celebrate the liturgy in a vital and transforming way, but find great difficulty in fulfilling this desire.

Older people
Older people often complain that they can no longer pray the Mass as they did before. They don't simply mean that they cannot say prayers at Mass but they no longer experience Mass as prayer. 'I know it's the same but somehow the mystery is gone out of it for me', they will tell you; or 'It doesn't seem to be sacred anymore'; or most simply, 'I don't know what to do at Mass any more'. Their difficulty was articulated for me rather poignantly a few years ago. After Mass in a hospital ward at which no-one answered the responses, an elderly gentleman

called me over and tried to explain their embarrassed silence. 'We're afraid to say anything now in case it might be wrong. I learned all the prayers when the Mass changed first: Glorias, Creeds and all, but these last changes have confused me and I'm afraid to say anything'. Indeed the same lack of enthusiasm for and confusion about the new translations are found among all age groups, the rhythm of the Gloria and Creed falters here and there and they 'raise/lift up' their hearts.

It would be a tragedy if we dismissed these statements as old-fashioned misunderstandings of what the new Mass is all about or as nostalgia for the old. There is a very genuine intuition and insight hidden in their deceptively simple words. They might not express it in these terms but this seems to be their genuine grievance. In the light of recent liturgical insights and developments we see that the old-style Latin Mass left a lot to be desired. Yet, despite the inadequacies of that liturgy as it was celebrated, today's senior citizens managed to share in the inner meaning of all liturgy. Whatever the priest might be saying or doing, they were remembering the life, death and resurrection of Jesus Christ (most often by meditating on the mysteries of the rosary) and relating that memory in a life-giving way to the joys and sorrows, the light and the darkness, the laughter and the tears of their daily lives.

Mass in Latin did not seem to relate to people's lives in any obvious way, but it did provide them with a sacred context, a sacred time and space within which they attempted to join every aspect of life to the living and transforming memory of Jesus Christ. This interlacing of their life-story and the history of Christ is what is essential to all liturgy. As David Power has pointed out, the 'harmonisation of opposites' at Mass facilitated the experience of mystery – there was deep silence and speech, seeing and not touching, distance and intimacy, divine majesty and the familiar ordinariness of everyday things. The simultaneous experience of all these realities by the whole person – mind, eyes, ears, nose – created an awesome atmosphere within which disclosure of mystery might take place. It also suggested different facets of the mystery and left plenty of scope for the religious imagination. By contrast, Mass today may seem to be all word and word only. Instead of trying obliquely to disclose something of the mystery we celebrate, it appears to be trying to transpose it whole and entire into dull, unimaginative, unpoetic words. Since they hear this kind of language being used in their churches, it is hardly surprising that people expect the meaning of the rites to be immediately available and intelligible.

Older people often complain about noise. So the 'noise of our solemn assembly' with its relentless barrage of words must assault their ears. And since every word is equally boosted, it becomes impossible to hear the more crucial words. It is no wonder that this group of people finds it difficult fully to inhabit the new liturgy and no-one has told them where they might make a beginning. Priests carry on as if it were all very obvious and are sometimes insensitive to feelings of loss and insecurity.

A middle group
Some sharp criticism of recent developments can be heard within groups of priests, clerical students, religious and vocal lay people. They recall their early fervour, the excitement of the first dawning of renewal, key ideas from the *Constitution* that held out so much promise. Phrases and slogans repeated often then, sound hollow now. 'Participate, participate, participate', a teacher said to me, 'and there is no participation'. The people of God were supposed 'to be able to understand the texts and rites with ease and take part in them fully, actively and as befits a community' (SC 21), but some have rather bitterly remarked that all they were ever told was that there were new changes and that these were the new responses. 'To take part in them fully', they insist, must mean more than making the responses, reading a lesson once every few months or years or sheepishly taking part in a mawkish 'offertory' procession. Minor modifications may have been introduced but it is still a liturgy for uninvolved spectators who watch someone else doing something for them out there. This is further aggravated if the president of the assembly treats the Mass as a text to be read rather than as an action to be celebrated.

They see too that much of what has percolated through to parish level seems to be concerned only with externals – with setting, with the techniques of ceremonial, with appearances. Of course these are indispensable, but they do not penetrate to the heart of the matter. It is a question of priorities. Re-arranging the dining-room tables does little to help a listing ship. People may be present at a model eucharist which is solemn, perfectly executed,

rubrically unimpeachable and yet be no more than distanced onlookers at a flawless performance. Some have unfairly described
the reforms as an exercise in 'liturgical archaeology', yet there
has been an over-emphasis on the study of texts and a definite
intellectualisation to the neglect of the non-textual, non-verbal
aspects, the whole world of symbol and sign. If liturgy means a
'work of the people', how can rites expressing living faith be de-
vised and decreed by 'experts'? Why wasn't more account taken
of the findings of the social sciences? Why the failure in collu-
sion between the editors of liturgy and the theorists of symbolic
action? It has also been noted that the past fifteen years witnessed the reversal of a direction that has always been present in
the history of liturgy – development from below being screened
and confirmed from above. Today, 'development' is imposed
from above without consultation.

Some members of this group who wish to study more about the
sacraments or discuss the liturgy, discover that the language
and ideas of the sacramental world are quaint and odd and at
times virtually unintelligible to the uninitiated. Even for those
who have studied theology, the inconsistency between the general trends of contemporary theology and the theology of sacraments is still unresolved.

The *Constitution* stated clearly that any hopes for full and active
participation by all the people would be futile 'unless pastors
themselves, to begin with, became thoroughly penetrated with
the spirit and power of the liturgy and become masters of it. It is
vitally necessary, therefore, that attention be directed, above all,
to the liturgical instruction of the clergy'. (SC 14) One could hardly
say that this has happened. Many priests will readily admit that
they know little enough about the liturgy, are not sure what 'celebration' means and are embarrassed now by the glib way they
spoke about 'participation' ten or twelve years ago. They know
too that they have paid lip-service only to the new insights into
the priesthood of the faithful and their own ministry of service to
that priestly people. At Mass they sometimes feel at a distance,
out of touch, like men going through the motions, unable to enter
into vital contact with their congregation. Some who are painfully
aware of these difficulties and the urgency of their task, want to
begin, even at this late hour, to learn together about the liturgy,
to discuss their difficulties, to celebrate Mass together so that
they might 'be aided to live the liturgical life and to share it with
the faithful entrusted to their care'. (SC 18)

Other priests say that they have studied liturgy, encouraged active participation, organised music and singing, yet the people still seem bored and listless and they themselves feel frustrated.

Young people
Finally, what are young people saying to us about their experience of worship? Jack Dominian highlighted some of the things to be kept in mind if we wish to speak of young people in the church:

> Catholics and Christians of other denominations are constantly comparing the church as they knew it before the council with the church of today. However, there is emerging with increasing force a church, mostly of young people, who know very little about the pre-conciliar church, who are in many ways different types of Christians and Roman Catholics. For them, many of the familiar arguments are boring, obsolete and irrelevant. They are conscious of totally new priorities which can be summed up first of all in their genuine difficulty in experiencing God; and secondly, when they do find this God, in their identification of his presence in the love of personal relationships and in social justice in the local community and in that of the deprived abroad. Love in personal relationships and social justice dominates the minds of the emerging church as apologetics, obeying rules and regulations, authoritarian principles and the salvation of one's soul, dominated the minds of a previous generation. For this emerging generation of believers, God's presence is to be acknowledged, not only directly through prayer, liturgy and the sacraments, but through the community of personal relationships and the wider community of peoples where the priority above all is social justice between those who have and those who have not. (*The Tablet*, 20 November, 1976)

Fifty per cent of the Irish population is under twenty-five years of age. This means that many young people were actually baptised into the reformed rites of the church and that the others retain, at most, a vague memory of the 'glories of the past'. Furthermore, according to the survey on 'Religious Practices', the non-attendance and noncommunicant rate among this age-group is well above the general figure. But, of those who continue to come regularly to Sunday Mass, many are serious about try-

ing to live Christianity, yet say that they find the liturgy boring
and monotonous. It is interesting to note that while their grand-
parents and even their parents tended to ask, 'What was said?',
they ask 'What happened?' They are not to be blamed if the answer is 'Not much'! However, this is not to say that they are
looking for 'happenings' or peak experiences at each eucharist.
Many are profoundly prayerful people who have a genuine criticism to make. Often idealistic themselves, they are very sensitive to a lack of this quality in others. The patent contradiction
between what people proclaim by participating in the eucharist
and what they actually do in daily life shocks them. If they see
no change, no attempt at transformation in the lives of those
who celebrate Mass, they begin to question the point of the
whole exercise: Why is there no consistency between the Sunday
half-hour and the rest of the week? How can you celebrate 'the
death of the Lord until he comes' and ignore the poor, the broken and the lonely? The dream 'to be rich and right with God' is
not yet their dream.

And is their criticism of the clergy a fair criticism? 'Why do you
never present the uncompromising challenge of Christianity to
the people?' 'If they use the sacraments like this they are hyp-
ocrites, yet you let them be; you do not take a stand. You offer
them cheap automatic grace which confirms them in their
hypocrisy. You are afraid to speak out in case they might stay
away because you are obsessed with numbers.' A rather irate
young woman put it more succinctly: 'All you priests care about
is getting as many people as possible into the church, giving
them communion as quickly as possible and clearing the place
for a new batch.' These criticisms strike home.

Common ground?
Does a common ground of difficulty emerge from the reactions
of our three groups? To generalise is to risk falsification, but
they seem to be saying that they find it difficult to recognise
themselves and their experience of life today in the liturgy as
they know it. They are searching for something which will enable them to read the joys and the tragedies, the throbbing experiences and the abrasive ordinariness of daily life in Christ-terms.
In their experience the liturgy does not seem to interpret, thematise and transform the mute, obscure contradictions of their
daily lives. It does not communicate deeply felt truth about the
agonising questions of life. Instead, they appear to be asked to

leave the profane world behind and enter into a fane but marginal world governed by arcane ground-rules. They are convinced that it should really speak to their lives, yet they say that they emerge unchanged. It does not help to tell them that the liturgy is concerned to break open their lives to the mystery of Christ; they are saying that they do not experience it in that way. The pastoral implications of this impasse are immense.

Note

1. This chapter was first published in *The Furrow*, January 1979.

CHAPTER 2

Liturgy: Transition and tradition [1]

Then we had nothing – neither a past
For precedent nor a future foreseeable
With the old ways ... we knew a kind of visible security
– The security of a familiar ritual.
(Desmond O'Grady, *The Old Way*)

These lines seem to catch something of the experience of insecurity, loss of identity and nostalgia for the past which can dominate during a period of upheaval and transition. We are living through a critical period of profound change at present and while its origins can be traced back into history, the dramatic character of developments since the 1950s is startling. Yet during these years, in the midst of this 'crisis of growth', the church was attempting the difficult task of renewing itself. The instability and confusion characteristic of modern life were bound to affect this renewal and to make that task at once more pressing and more difficult.

It was indispensable that the church proclaim the mystery of Christ in a renewed way to people who were actually living through these painful changes. A new transforming vision of God and of the depth and purpose of human life must be offered so that people might 'christen their wild-worst best'(Hopkins) by being enabled to bind together the past, present and future and interpret them in a hope-full and reconciling way. The church has always attempted to do this most concretely and most intensively through its liturgy. 'It is the outstanding means whereby the faithful may express in their lives and manifest to others the mystery of Christ and the real nature of the true church'. (SC 2) And now that liturgy had to be renewed. However if the people were finding it difficult to cope with change in all other areas of their lives, they might be tempted to look to the church for some kind of absolute, immutable stability.

Renewal and change in the old familiarities of church life might well be confusing and threatening to those who hankered after a haven, a bastion or a comfort zone. Since a 'gloriously unchanging liturgy' seemed to epitomise all that was best in the traditional way of life, renewal of the forms of worship might prove very traumatic indeed. 'Then we had nothing ... '

The lesson of history
Such difficulties and tensions have of course accompanied the liturgical renewal so far, and as time goes on others continue to emerge. Accordingly, some commentators have felt justified in saying that the sacramental life of the church has entered a crisis in recent years. While this may be true, it is necessary to keep things in perspective by remembering that this is not the first time that a crisis over worship has been experienced within the Judaeo-Christian tradition. A random overview of its history seems to indicate that significant cultural shifts have nearly always caused heart-searching and uncertainty about worship.

In Israel the cultural change involved in moving from a nomadic to a settled way of life gave rise to certain difficulties. The pilgrim symbols of exodus, the covenant-commitment, the story, the meal, were difficult to maintain among a people now dependent on the fertility of a definite piece of land. New symbols, more characteristic of settled life, enter the Jewish vocabulary: the king, the palace, the temple and its cycle of sacrifices, the festivals, the detailed laws. The dangers in such a transition became clear when the prophets fulminated against the decadence and formalism of Israel's worship. Later the violent break in the established order during the exile gave rise to a quite different emphasis in worship which concentrated on the Book and the liturgy of the word. The radical breakthrough towards which Jesus of Nazareth was leading his followers embodied itself in renewed ritual action and interpretative words celebrating the new exodus into freedom and the new covenant with God.

In the Christian era it seems that the varying emphases in worship-forms down the centuries, more or less reflect the position of the church within the dominant culture. One thinks of the contrast between the little groups exiled from both Judaism and the Empire meeting 'at dawn to hymn Christ as a God' and the

post-Constantinian status of the church within the Empire reflected in solemn, ordered liturgies and embodied in the stone of
basilicas and cathedrals. As the medieval world changed, it
adopted and adapted the rituals of the early church, thereby
changing what it preserved. In the West the period between
1350 and 1750 was a period of major transition, influenced
above all by the Renaissance, the Reformation and the Counter-
Reformation and they left their distinctive marks on the liturgy.
The new vision of the Reformation churches and their relationship to society and tradition, found expression in a renewed emphasis in covenant, fellowship and the power of the word of
God. The Tridentine liturgical reforms were to hold sway for 400
years, yet social conditions could still necessitate modifications –
the influence of the Penal Laws on the celebration of the liturgy
in Ireland is a case in point.

The situation today
With this lesson in history before us, we realise that if men and
women today understand themselves and their world in a new
way, if society is celebrating the death of permanence, if the
mythic, poetic, and symbolic dimensions of life are being eroded,
this is bound to have a profound effect on the whole question of
worship. Given the contemporary fragmentation of social structures, questions about the purpose of worship, about its possibility, its relationship to life, its structures, were inevitable. It could
never have been a question of averting a crisis, but of enabling
people to cope more effectively with it. Even with hindsight it is
not easy to say how this might have been achieved.

For the present, however, I wish to concentrate on a more specific
question. If the problems and difficulties outlined in the previous chapter really exist, we must ask: what are the prospects for
worship today? This is not just a theoretical question, rather it is
posed as a painful, agonising question by many people – how
can we continue to worship, how can we return to it if we have
ceased to 'practise'? All of us must ask ourselves from time to
time whether we can participate more fully in the liturgy, can
we celebrate it as we should in a vibrant and transforming way?

Take our celebration of the eucharist on Sunday in any given
parish. It may be far from the ideal. There are many things

which could be improved, problems which could be overcome. Perhaps if we had more involvement in the liturgy of the word, more hymns, a more dignified procession of the gifts, a new altar, better microphones ... Perhaps. These things are important, but sooner or later we will have to ask: with what kind of model of eucharistic celebration are we working here? Are we working from the outside and saying in effect, 'If we read this leaflet, sing these hymns, stand up at this time, say these responses, we will experience what the liturgy is'? If we see it like this, it is hardly surprising that Sunday Mass seems extrinsic to our lives, for we have been tackling our problem backwards. We must begin instead from the inside, by starting with ourselves and with other people. To take this seriously, we would have to be convinced that the eucharist is not just a spectacle to be looked at, it is relevant to our lives, for this *is* our life. Here, the scattered, unedited fragments of our daily living and dying are being joined in a transforming way to the memorial of Jesus Christ. If we were convinced that this is what liturgy is, if we saw how it related to our lives, if we understood something of the subversive and reconciling power of the eucharist, if we were prepared to let it call us into question and change our lives, I believe we would want to participate as fully as possible – we might even want to sing!

I am suggesting that part of our trouble comes from the inadequacy of our model or image of what constitutes a eucharistic celebration. Our basic difficulty lies at the level of our own interpretation and presentation of the eucharist and not with the reality of the eucharist in itself. We tend to work with a single model or interpretation of the eucharist, which we regard as absolutely sacrosanct and immutable, and so we suffer from a self-inflicted impoverishment. It is easy to diminish the fullness of the eucharistic mystery if we do not take account of the wealth, variety and diversity of our liturgical heritage. The history of the eucharist shows us that the cultural situation in which the church found herself at any given time had a profound influence on what would be emphasised when she gathered to celebrate the sacred mysteries. If we forget this, we may find ourselves trying to continue a given historical emphasis in a world that is radically different, thereby ignoring these aspects of the eucharistic mystery which should be emphasised for our own contemporaries. I am not at all suggesting that we should break with tradition. On

the contrary I am maintaining that we should cherish and explore
the depth and richness of that tradition in a time of transition.

Perhaps what I am trying to say might become clearer if I were
briefly to outline, out of many available, three models or approaches to the celebration of the eucharist. They are not new,
they have always been in existence, but if they could be recovered, they would, I believe, enable us to bring certain necessary
emphases to bear on the painful questions which some people
have about worship today.

The Emmaus model

The narrative in Luke 24:13 gives an account of two people who
had been disciples of Jesus of Nazareth. Their hopes have been
dashed, he whom they followed is now dead, the liberator has
been crucified and in their sad disappointment they experience
only his absence and death. 'They stood still looking sad'. (v 17)
I think many people can recognise themselves in the reactions of
these two former disciples. Jesus Christ had once been of ultimate significance for them, the Christian faith had made sense of
life and death but a change came and they know now only the
absence of Christ. Worship no longer interprets life or mediates
meaning so they cannot take part in it because it seems to take
for granted precisely what has been painfully called into question for them. They can no longer celebrate 'the death of the Lord
until he comes' for they only know his death and cannot hope
for his coming. Yet the memory of Christ will not let them be. It
is impossible to excise completely what had been so much a part
of their living selves; their hearts are still burning within them.

What do we say to them? Do we let them be? Perhaps we must
first of all see ourselves in the portrait of these two disciples.
Christianity assures us that God's final word to humankind is an
utterly gracious, merciful and hope-full word, that God has definitively taken humanity to himself in the flesh and blood of
Jesus Christ. This is the 'good news' that we beings-for-death
need to hear proclaimed over and over again in the eucharist.
Having celebrated the constant presence of Christ to us in daily
life, having recognised in a visible way the hidden Christ who
always walks with us, we are asked to go forth from each eucharistic moment of recognition more sensitive to this hidden

presence of Christ in everyone we meet and in 'the bits and pieces of every day'. I have been emphasising the word 'recognition', for in the Emmaus story we are told 'that their eyes were opened and they recognised him' (v 31) in the taking, blessing, breaking and giving of bread and they understood the real significance of the burning in their hearts.

If we believe that Christianity began because forgiveness and reconciliation were offered by the Risen Christ to disciples whose discipleship had been called into question by his death, we will feel compelled to offer that same forgiveness and reconciliation to his present-day former disciples by bringing them to this moment of recognition. If we could allow this compulsion to influence our celebration of the eucharist, it would speak more effectively to those who recognise themselves in the feeling and reactions of the two disciples. It demands great sensitivity, but the fact that we are willing to make the attempt itself speaks volumes. It says, first of all and most importantly, that we empathise with their situation and are not trying to impose something on them from the outside. The liturgy, we are declaring, is reaching out to them where they are, is reaching for their hearts and is attempting to interpret the now anonymous burning which is there and will not go away. They are still seeking stability, coherence, direction and meaning in life, but they cannot any longer accept that Christianity offers what they seek. However, it is about Christianity *as it was presented to them* that they make this judgement, so the onus is on us to show them that the authentic face of Christ may have been hidden from them through misunderstanding – 'But their eyes were kept from recognising him'. (v 16) We must be able to show how Christianity, rightly understood, can interpret and thematise their life-experiences in Christ-terms by offering reconciliation and repentance – 'Always be prepared to make defence to any one who calls you to account for the hope that is in you, yet do it with gentleness and reverence'. (1 Pet 3:15) Finally, without being paternalistic, we would have to say that while they think of themselves as 'post-Christian', we believe that they are still Emmaus disciples who are loved unconditionally by Jesus Christ and with whom he constantly walks as the ever-present but hidden Lord.

Table-fellowship model[2]

The gospels present Jesus to us as someone captivated by the mystery of the loving graciousness of God whom he addresses as Abba. He wishes to speak of the passionate love of Abba for all men and women and is constantly struggling to communicate this insight to his hearers. If only they could be given a glimpse into the mystery of the Father's love, if only they could be brought face to face with it, even for a moment, everything would be achieved. To experience the sheer boundless generosity of God's mercy and forgiveness was to be blessed indeed and to know the beginning of a new way of life. So in his parables and in his preaching we see him struggling to find the most striking and most powerful image possible to disclose the love of this Prodigal Father to them. This preaching met with incomprehension and open hostility because it seemed to overturn so many of the common certainties of religious life. The contemporary moral ethic proclaimed that if men and women repented then God would forgive them. Jesus seemed in effect to be reversing this value system completely and to be saying: show them that God loves them even though they are sinners, help them to appreciate the true character of his love and forgiveness and then they will repent. He scandalised the pious Jews of his time by offering salvation to notorious sinners whom they avoided as a religious duty. The good news of God's gracious benevolence was being proclaimed by Jesus to the poor, the sinner, the wounded, the simple, 'the sat upon, spat upon, ratted on people' of society who had previously understood themselves as eternally cut off from salvation. His mission was to reveal the sheer prodigality of the Father's love to such people and to bring them to recognise God as he truly is. Those who understood their true position before God, their utter need for forgiveness, could understand and appreciate Jesus' scandalous message. There was room for God in their lives. 'We must be nothing, nothing that God may make us something ... God must be allowed to surprise us ...' ('Having Confessed', P. Kavanagh).

However Jesus was not content merely to speak about the love and mercy of Abba. He wished to translate this teaching into action as well. He wanted his followers to experience this gift of the Father in the most complete, most palpable, most fully human way possible and he did this by engaging in unrestricted table-fellowship. He chose this medium to proclaim forgiveness

in the most dramatic way possible. Jesus, a 'glutton and a drunkard, a friend of tax-collectors and sinners' (Luke 7:34) excluded
no one from his meals. For a Jew to take part in a meal meant fellowship with God and fellowship with those who sat at table.
Those who broke bread together shared in the blessing of God
pronounced over the elements of the meal, and Jesus invited 'the
sinner and the righteous' to share it together. So we begin to
realise that eating and drinking in the company of Jesus can only
be understood in terms of theology and eschatology. By drawing sinners into table-fellowship with himself, he was making a
powerful statement about God and his final salvation. He dared
to offer hope to the hopeless in the name of God. His self-righteous contemporaries were fiercely scandalised at this offensive
behaviour of offering divine forgiveness, brotherhood and
sisterhood to people whom they excluded from the liturgical
assemblies. They knew that he was overturning the values by
which they lived their lives and their understanding of merit,
'and they took offence at him'. (Mark 6:3) They would not allow
God to be God and looked on him rather as a keeper of accounts.
Jesus had to oppose them because they were convinced that
their understanding of the law coincided with God's true demands and because of this they prevented the 'little ones', the
true heirs of the kingdom, from coming to their Father.

We must allow this emphasis to influence our eucharistic celebration as well. The same deep concern for the outcast and the
sinner must drive us to search out those who do not come to our
assemblies or who stand at their margins so that we may seat
them once again at the Father's table. The table-fellowship of our
eucharists must mediate the prodigal love of God to all who assemble there.

Parable model[3]
Jesus proclaimed the kingdom of God in the haunting, disturbing and unforgettable poetics that we call his parables. They are
not some kind of teaching aid or means of instruction used by
Jesus, they are a form of proclamation. He has poured himself
into the parables to such an extent that ultimately he will die for
the truth they proclaim. Although the stories themselves apparently speak about the trivialities of daily life, yet the listeners are
forced to become part of the parables of the kingdom and freed

to decide for or against the total reversal of values that they un-
fold. No easy solutions are offered. They do not coerce or cajole.
At most, they provide a framework for thinking things through.
They bring the hearers towards a new realisation or launch them
in a new direction but they can never bring to completion what
has been begun in them. The simplicity and directness of the
parables mean that they can challenge everyone, no matter what
their social, religious or educational background may be. They
are symbolic probes that dig into each person's life where they
are at. Suddenly a person is asked to re-examine everything that
had previously been taken for granted, to reverse the accepted
judgements of common sense and to begin to live in a new way.
The parables can mediate an experience of the kingdom of God
so dramatically that one cannot be a passive, uninvolved listener,
one cannot even hesitate. Ultimately the hearer is challenged to
accept or reject Jesus and his God.

We need to apply something of the power of the parables to our
celebration of the eucharist. The challenge of the paradoxical
mystery of the life, death and resurrection of Jesus Christ must
be allowed to touch our lives and to call us into question. Do the
values proclaimed in the liturgy of the word and in the eucharistic
prayer really confront the values we enshrine in our daily lives?
If the death of Jesus Christ was the direct consequence of the
consistency of his life, then the eucharist as his memorial must
probe the consistency of our lives.

Conclusion

If we could allow the power in these three models to influence
our celebration of the eucharist, we might have the beginnings
of an answer for those whose basic criticism of liturgy is their inability to recognise themselves and their experience of life in it.
We should be able to show them that because the eucharist is
about the life, death and resurrection of Jesus Christ, which
alone makes sense of any life, then no life and no facet of life can
be foreign to the eucharist. In other words, without any change
in its structure, without innovations or gimmicks, we should be
able to involve people by showing them how it relates to their
lives. To do this we have to explore the full range of possibilities
available within the New Order of Mass and try to inhabit them
in a creative and imaginative way. (On a much more elementary
level, how many priests confine themselves each day to the

same form of the greeting, penitential rite, the prayers of the faithful, preparation of the gifts, preface or proclamation?) When we become aware of the richness available to us, it is then a question of sensitively discovering the points of deepest contact between the lives of a particular congregation and the Mass. Here the priest has to carry out the vital ministry of translating, interpreting and establishing bridges between life and liturgy. This ministry will be effective and credible only to the extent that he has previously exercised it in their homes and places of work. Arranging an entrance rite for people on Sunday will not overcome the failure to enter into their lives during the week.

Of course, the practical question of how to achieve this kind of celebration with the mass of people who gather together on Sundays arises immediately. The truthful answer is that it is extremely difficult. However, the fact that we do not have an impact on all should not deter us from allowing the penitential rite, the liturgy of the word, the homily and the eucharistic prayer to be as effective as possible. However, the table-fellowship and parable models have very obvious applications, especially in the context of small group-liturgies. At such a liturgy the sharing of the Body and Blood of Christ takes place within a wider sharing of life and love. It attempts to deepen the genuine community already existing among people whose daily lives mingle and meld, by proclaiming Christ to be the ultimate source of all unity. Liturgy and life become linked in a very powerful way when the eucharist is celebrated in the very place where the joys and sorrows, pain and suffering of human life are experienced. 'Today salvation has come to this house' (Luke 19:10) takes on a new meaning when people gather for Mass in their own homes, among family, friends and neighbours to whom they are already open and receptive and through whom they are already responding to Christ. It is a matter of trying to discover prayer-situations in people's lives, of knowing the moments when they are especially open to the message of Christianity and of relating the good news of Christ to these experiences. Such moments arise when death comes to young or old, when sickness blights, when significant stages are reached in the family, in school or in work, when exile or homecoming fill the heart. Such experiences, and the abrasive ordinariness of daily living, cry out to be read and interpreted in the light of Jesus Christ. 'In a crumb of bread the whole mystery is'.

Yet we cannot concentrate on small groups only, because if the liturgy is to reflect the rhythm of life today, there is need for small intimate groupings and larger assemblies. If parish life were characterised by both, then our experience of Sunday Mass would be quite different. Sunday congregations would not be gatherings of more or less isolated individuals, but the assembly of a number of cohesive groups who had celebrated the eucharist together during the week, and had been transformed by the experience. When this possibility has been actualised, we will have gone a long way towards fulfilling the hopes and dreams of those who wish to renew the liturgy. We may even have begun to meet the deepest needs of the people of God.

Notes

1. This chapter was first published in *The Furrow*, January 1980.

2. See *New Testament Theology*, vol 1, J. Jeremias (SCM 1971).

3. See the vast literature available on parables, especially J. D. Crossan, *In Parables*, Harper and Row, 1974.

CHAPTER 3

Cult and our apathetic culture [1]

Are modern people even capable
of responding to liturgical symbols?
(Romano Guardini)

Faced with the trauma and upheaval of the years immediately following the council, some Catholics were saddened and at times angered to find that the renewed liturgy no longer offered tranquil succour. Others, rejoicing in their new acceptance of change, were impatient with the gradualism and inconsistencies of the liturgical renewal and its apparent inability to facilitate the quest for meaning and hope in life itself. Many others accepted what had been proposed with bemused obedience.

But beyond the diversity of response and beyond the unevenness and dissonance of the renewal process itself, most Catholics would agree that they now have access to an experience of liturgy that is incomparably richer than that of the preconciliar days. We can point to the success of the vernacular in the liturgy, to the growing appreciation of the corporate nature of worship and the meaning of 'active participation', to the restoration to the laity of a variety of ministries of word and eucharist, to the extraordinary change in the practice of frequent communion. (Do you remember the servers looking around to see if anyone was 'coming to the rails'?) At another level, we have begun to probe the nature of communication in the liturgy, especially at the non-verbal level and to pay attention to symbol, ritual and imagination. We realise too that true participation in the liturgy demands conversion, because the difficulties we have with the liturgy reside not only in the liturgy and celebration but above all in ourselves.

On the negative side, people express disappointment and frustration with church leadership and fear that the renewal is still vulnerable to authoritarian dictat. Disappointment too is voiced about many priests' understanding of liturgy and scripture, about their style of presidency of the assembly and about the deplorable quality of so much preaching. The failure of people at prayer to link liturgy and social justice, to acknowledge the cry of the poor, to protest against the poverty, squalor and degradation of millions of human beings is a great scandal to some.

Questions about women and liturgy, about the difficulties of adaptation and inculturation, about the significance of seeing a liturgical assembly as a group, and so on, have only begun to be addressed. Much work remains to be done. Indeed some commentators suggest that we are just now in a position to read the *Constitution* and to think seriously about renewing the liturgy! Be that as it may, no approach to the liturgy can afford to ignore the relationship between liturgy and culture.

In 1962 Romano Guardini asked: 'Are modern people even capable of responding to liturgical symbols?' He was suggesting that the problem with liturgy for very many people was a problem of culture. The intervening years have shown the accuracy of his insight. As the title of this chapter suggests, I think the question 'How are we to worship a Passionate Christ in the midst of our apathetic culture?' is the fundamental question which we need to tackle if we are to face the challenge of celebrating liturgy today. I would like to offer some reflections on certain aspects of this question. But first of all, why do I pose the question in these terms?

I would want the word 'passionate' to evoke the sense of something strong and vibrant yet straining towards completion, restless and concentrated towards some crucial breakthrough. It has overtones of violence yet its root meaning connotes submission and suffering and endurance in the quest for what is desired, without counting the cost. I want to use this extraordinarily rich word, with all its possible connotations, to speak of what characterises the entire life, ministry and message of Jesus the Christ. I want it to convey the sense of his passionate and scandalous involvement with all kinds of people. I want it to announce his passionate and challenging involvement as Risen Lord in the heart of our lives and our worship.[2]

By way of contrast, I use the word 'apathetic' to call to mind what lacks passion, what is dull, listless, uninterested, what rests satisfied with what is, what ignores or denies the need for breakthrough, what is indifferent, insensitive to the suffering of others and does not care what happens to them. It is that listlessness, that withdrawal of energy, that distancing from the other, that fatalism, that passivity, I have in mind in choosing this word. The word describes those who are convinced that they have just enough energy to sustain their own existence, to look after their own private interests, who refuse to become involved, who experience only a perverted passion for the self, who refuse to accept that their apathetic stance towards life has repercussions on the lives of others. This is the word I have chosen to name what I regard as a fundamental malaise of our culture today and which profoundly affects our engagement in liturgy.

I should say that I am using the word 'culture' in a very wide, non-technical sense, almost as a synonym for 'our world', or simply 'the way people live'. I am thinking in particular of the mindset, the whole frame of reference within which we experience and interpret life today. And I am suggesting that much of it is inimical to what should be happening when we gather 'to proclaim the death of the Lord until he comes'.

When church people try to explain why things are as they are today, they often appeal to the old scapegoats of secularism, materialism and consumerism. There is, of course, truth in the appeal that our secular age is materialistic and consumerist – but it is not the whole truth. Rather we need to ask: Where do we locate ourselves as we make this judgement about our world – outside or inside society? Otherwise this talk about the evils of today's world can easily become a thinly disguised form of self-righteousness: 'These terrible trends have been brought about by irreligious people, but thank God we don't have hand, act or part in them. All we innocents can do is wring our hands as we helplessly stand by'.

Even if we were innocent, our role is not to bemoan but rather to find imaginative and positive ways of living and celebrating the Christian vision in today's world. But, of course, we are not innocent. None of us is vacuum-sealed from the world around us. It penetrates into the heart of every sanctuary and invades the sanctuary of the heart. We are inescapably involved in the local and global situation and we must accept responsibility for the part we play in it. Many of us find these insights difficult to accept. Often we only get as far as saying: 'Yes, we live in this kind of world and yes, it does influence us to a certain extent, but it's really Christianity that is the true guiding force in my life.' It would be wonderful to be able to say that and really mean it, but what does the evidence of daily life suggest?

We know that it is possible to say that Christianity is our real guide only when a passionate faith in Jesus Christ orders our total experience, creates a new world for us and for others, when following him dominates our imaginations and actions. Yet how many of us could claim that this is an accurate description of our day-to-day lives? Writers on sociology and the philosophy of religion maintain that this should not surprise us. They tell us that society socialises people, it creates the mind-set out of which people perceive, understand and respond to their world and according to which they act. So the social structures of society, the political institutions, the economic systems, the modes of production, have a profound influence on the socialisation process, the worldview and the very mental make-up of people. Not only do they influence us from outside, rather it seems that they enter into and condition the structures of our consciousness, the structures of our imagination, our basic mind-set, our guiding vision of life. Consequently they condition the values and the motivations that determine our responses to the world around us. If this is true, then the consequences are frightening both for our lives and for our liturgies.

Is it true? Let us take the influence of television on us as an example. TV, more powerfully and persuasively than any other medium, provides the collective images, stereotypes, myths and ideologies of popular culture today. And as someone said, 'You don't have to be tuned in to be wired up' – even if you never watch TV its influence is still reaching us through the people who do! Images from TV can haunt people, oppress them, penetrate their patterns of thought and emotion, not so much directly and overtly as indirectly and subliminally. It has the capacity to absorb, tame and trivialise. For millions of people time is not only organised around the TV programme schedule but their very perception of time is changed. Helena Sheehan puts it this way:

> Television has brought far-reaching and fundamental changes,

not only in how we spend our time, but in how we perceive our world, how we codify our experiences, how we relate to others and how we respond to other media. It not only occupies more of the waking hours of more of the world's population than any other medium in history, but it has probably reconstructed irrevocably our whole sensory apparatus. It surely has altered the nature of our sensory balance in that it represents a return, though on a new level, to a culture that is more oral and visual than literary. ... It has brought the decline of modes of perception and expression that are more contemplative, more analytical, more synthetic, more deeply rooted, more enduring ...

It can condition the mind to constant cutting, discontinuity and disruption, pushing the span of attention and power of concentration to near the vanishing point, and making the flow of consciousness and sense of personal identity as jagged and as fractured as the flow of television. ... It can breed cynicism and disillusion, with the weight of the unending stream of palpable falsity.[3]

If this kind of change is being brought about in the structures of our minds and imaginations by many forces in society today, we can only guess at the consequences for human beings in the world.

Since the material conditions of life, the place people occupy in it, the cultural expressions and so on, have such an influence on the way we perceive and respond to the world around us, we have to accept that our guiding vision, our basic life structure, is never wholly created by our religious tradition. Rather it may be formed by even stronger social, economic, political and cultural factors. Social analysts maintain, though at first hearing it may sound surprising, that religion is always, for most people, a secondary socialisation process. They see religion as either conforming to what has been given in society or as seeking to modify it. (Perhaps this throws some light on the different forms of estrangement from the church that we find among both the 'churched' and the 'unchurched'.)

Because the very culture we inhabit is as it is, because it seems to drain so much human energy to merely survive, what is left for the struggle that is necessary if Christianity is to be more than a secondary socialising process? Can we seek to modify the givens

of society? Do we have the energy or the will to resist being
swamped by the alluring idols of our apathetic culture that
promise life but deal only in death? If the dominant culture so
enters into our minds and hearts and souls, it would take enor-
mous energy and resources to resist it, for it would mean living
in a counter-cultural way. It would require a deep, on-going
conversion, a struggle with 'principalities and powers', to ensure
that the following of Jesus Christ be the primary focus of life. Yet
that is what is needed if the Passionate Christ is to be allowed to
mould our lives and transform our liturgies.

To enquire about whether or how such a counter-cultural approach
might be possible is to enquire about our basic spirituality! It
means asking not simply how do we pray, but what is our basic
spirituality? Michael Warren stresses that, 'A spirituality is a
way of walking, a particular way of being in the world. It is entirely possible to have two conflicting spiritualities, a verbal or
notional one, which we might claim guides our lives, and the
lived one, which is the actual one. The first is an illusory spirituality, which is named and not lived, but which belies the actual
spirituality, which is lived but not always named. Thus it is possible to claim in verbal declaration that we have a Christian spirituality, whereas the actual way we structure our lives right down
to our simplest decisions is not based on the gospel at all.'[4]

If this kind of ambivalence exists at the level of our spirituality,
what happens when we 'prepare to celebrate the sacred mysteries?' Liturgy is not magic. We may be very close to the situation
that St Paul critiqued in the Corinthian community, which had
conformed itself to the Corinthian culture but claimed to be authentically celebrating the Christ cult. Are we prepared to heed
his call to 'examine ourselves'? Are we prepared to say where
we really invest our interest and energy, knowing that there too
'our hearts' are to be found? It is this giving of the heart that tells
both ourselves and others what our real basic Credo (*Cor dare*) is.
Is it given over to the Passionate Christ or conformed to our
apathetic culture? The honest answers to these questions will
determine what happens when we take part in the Christ cult.

Notes

1. This chapter was first published in the Newsletter of the Catechetical Association of Ireland, Autumn 1988.

2. See Haughton, R., *The Passionate God*, DLT 1981.

3.This paragraph has drawn on H. Sheehan's, *Irish TV Drama*, RTE, 1987.

4. 'Catechesis and Spirituality', *Religious Education*, Winter 1988.

CHAPTER 4

Thirty years on

We must be still and still moving
to another intensity.
(T S Eiot)

'In Bologna, on the titular feast of a convent where his sister was abbess, Pope Benedict XIV celebrated the pontifical High Mass. The nuns had practiced their most beautiful Mass and in the sung creed the words 'begotten not made' were repeated in endless variations. Irritated by this warbling, the Pope turned around in the middle of their singing and in a deep voice chanted, 'Begotten or made, the peace of the Lord be always with you'. Then he began the offertory.' I read these words[1] in the early months of 1969 and was amused by this expression of papal relativism.

Some months later, a few days after ordination, together with family and neighbours I celebrated the eucharist in my birth place. Afterwards, as I knelt in the little chapel, a woman whom I knew to be deeply devoted to daily eucharist was preparing to leave. As she was passing by she leaned towards me and said, 'I hope you say your prayers well, Father, for you don't half say the Mass.' I was not amused.

Later I discovered that the priest of the area had not begun to use the 'new' eucharistic prayers, so compared with the English translation of the Roman Canon, Eucharistic Prayer II must indeed have seemed like half a Mass! With that thought, at any rate, I consoled myself.

Both these stories have come to mind many times during the intervening years, and what took place between the actants has served as a summary of certain aspects of what has been happening in relation to liturgy during that time. They may also provide headings for these musings on the liturgy thirty years into the renewal. I might list them as: clerical leadership and the 'reception' of the reforms; spirituality and liturgy; popular religiosity and liturgy; women and liturgy; and, everpresent to the actants, powerfully conditioning their attitudes and responses even if unacknowledged by them, culture and context.

I will argue that the most crucial question in liturgical renewal has been and remains that of the relationship between culture and liturgy. I will try to show how that relationship impinges on the various topics dealt with in this chapter. I will suggest that to face the cultural question would mean implementing what has already been proclaimed in official documents, studying the nature of popular religiosity and ensuring that ongoing renewal takes account of the foundational nature of ritual and symbol.

The global context
In discussing liturgy, it is tempting to concentrate on what happens in actual celebrations at the parish level. Yet to do this runs the risk of ignoring the powerful, formative influences already at work in the lives of those who assemble there. It seems necessary to begin by indicating something of that broader canvas.

As we approach the third millenium, those who avidly scan the megatrends of our rapidly changing world offer us quite divergent master-images with which to interpret that world – some brightly optimistic, others darkly pessimistic.

Out of the fragmentation and insecurity that accompany the death-throes of the old familiar culture and the brooding birth-pangs of its successor, some social commentators maintain that they can discern already the emergence of a brave new world. That emergence, they say, is characterised by a new sense of our relatedness to one another, to the world, to creation and by a new unified vision of humanity. They point to the recent reframing of relations between East and West; the demise of communism; the renewed worldwide concern for human rights; the growing conviction about social justice and the integrity of creation; the initiatives in the Middle East; the significance and achievements of the women's movement; the implications of the Maastricht treaty, as evidence that slowly but inexorably we are becoming one world. They acknowledge the challenges that face the so-called advanced industrial societies at the social, economic, political, and even spiritual levels, as they become post-industrial, post-technological, post-modernist. But they have every confidence that we will not only survive these challenges but will achieve a breakthrough to a new transforming way of being human together.

The other group of commentators do not share this optimism or the (to them) overweening confidence of its proponents. By contrast they point to the constant miasma of war and suffering and death and destruction that has plagued this century and continues to characterise its final decade. Two world wars, more than one hundred million dead through war and violence, millions of refugees, twenty million needless deaths each year through hunger, famine and easily-preventable disease. As further evidence they remind us that, even with strategic arms limitation, we have enough nuclear warheads still to destroy the earth and its inhabitants fifteen or twenty times over and that the threat of a nuclear holocaust through war or accident is always hanging over us.

They point to the appalling, on-going destruction of human dignity through racism and sexism. They note that there has been no reframing of north-south relations in our world nor is there likely to be; that the 'structures of plunder' are still firmly in place; that the poor and hungry, two-thirds of the world's population, continue to become poorer and hungrier; that the quality of life has deteriorated for three quarters of humankind in the twentieth century. They remind us that half a billion people are starving, one billion are living in absolute poverty, one and a half billion are without even the most basic medical care. They are alarmed at the implications of increasing international and multinational competitivness and worry about whose interests the ongoing revolutions in technology will serve ultimately. They are gravely concerned at the lethal combination of pathological concern for the self and deadly apathy that has characterised so many lives in the 'developed world' through the grim crises of the 70s and the flourishing of the 'me-generation' of the 80s, when 'greed was creed'. They do not expect this situation to improve in the 90s when capitalism appears to have not merely the last but the only word.

They paint nightmare scenarios of the outcome of the AIDS crisis, of the information explosion that is already out of control, of the consequences of the pollution of sea and sky, of the destruction of the rainforests and the cataclysmic travail of mother earth herself. They believe that the implications of all of this are so serious that the human species and the human enterprise itself are what are ultimately at risk.

Even if the more positive interpretation is the one which most appeals to us, the presence of all the factors and forces mentioned by both sets of commentators, impinges on our lives in myriad ways. What then are we to say to these challenges presented to our very humanity by today's world? What are Christians to say in the name of a passionate Christ who lived and died that all might have life and have it to the full? What can we say when we gather to proclaim in memorial the death of that Christ until he comes?

The local context
The distinction being made here between global and local contexts is permeable, for the global situation is ever present to us in our daily lives through the mass media or in the very air that we breathe! Those worldwide concerns should impinge most sharply on us when we see them reflected in the Irish situation. Yet most of us manage not to be appalled, for example, at the maintenance on our behalf of the obscenity of meat and butter mountains in a world of hunger.

Our own unique set of shameful statistics continues to haunt us: 3,000 people killed through violence in Northern Ireland, 1,000,000 poor in the Irish Republic, close to 300,000 unemployed, 40% of the children of the nation living in homes subsisting below the poverty line, 25% of the youthful, well-educated, articulate population forced to emigrate. By the turn of the decade we had begun to resign ourselves to some of the consequences of the greedy 80s and the pragmatism and expediency that characterised public life. We had investigations and tribunals, there were rumours about white-collar crime and innuendo about sharp practises in business and accusations about self-aggrandisement in political and corporate affairs. But with the strange convergence of events in 1992, these matters seemed to reach a definite nadir with revelations concerning feet of clay within the 'golden circle' and on the episcopal bench. This generated a sense of confusion and bewilderment among many people. The disillusionment at what seemed like the dissolution of the last, common certainties went very deep indeed. It was felt that these revelations were not only symptomatic of what was happening in Irish society but were representative as well. The debate surrounding the X case raised again the questions about abortion, moral insight and the law that had been festering since the 1983 amendment. That debate in turn dictated, in large measure, the parameters of the discussion on Maastricht. So an opportunity to explore the challenge presented to our cultural, political, social, religious, moral and historical identity in the pluralism which is Europe, was lost. In the end we were left with little more than vapid generalisations and financial carrots to speed us in to full membership of the European Community or, as it is now called, European Union.

The other statistics
It has been fashionable over the past few years to talk about the 'crisis facing the church in Ireland' or 'à la carte Catholicism, Irish-style' and no doubt a considerable body of evidence could be advanced to support such assertions. But what are we to make of the statistics about the persistence of religious practice in Ireland which, at first sight anyway, seem to be at odds with those generalisations? The magic figure of 91% weekly Mass attendance in 1974 had fallen to 87% by 1984 and to 82% by 1989. Nevertheless that most recent statistic was far above the figure confidently and gloomily predicted for the 1990s fifteen years earlier. It is also noteworthy that during the period in question weekly reception of communion rose from 28% in 1974 to 43% in 1989.

These figures indicate that, statistically, Irish people's presence at and involvement in the eucharist, is far beyond that of any other country from which such statistics are available. But while these statistics tell us that more than 4 out of 5 Irish Catholics attend Mass weekly (and many of the remainder attend on some Sundays) they cannot tell us why the figures for Ireland are so different or what they really mean. No such interpretation is as yet available for the Irish situation, but we may be able to learn something from an important colloquium held at Georgetown University in the US to mark the 25th anniversary of the promulgation of the *Constitution on the Sacred Liturgy* of Vatican II (*The*

Awakening Church, L.J. Madden, The Liturgical Press, 1992). That colloquium was based on a study of the liturgy in fifteen parishes, from a variety of States, conducted by four US Liturgical Centres. These parishes were selected because they had demonstrated a sustained interest in implementing the reforms of the liturgy. Indeed the impression is given that these 'best' parishes also put on 'special' liturgies for the survey and we must note that figures for the reception of communion range from 85% to 99%.

Several speakers commented on the recurrence of words like 'warmth', 'closeness', 'comfortable', 'feeling good' in the survey to describe what was judged to be important in a 'good liturgy'. Some feared that, from the evidence available, the time of gathering and welcoming at the beginning of the celebration or the exchange of peace itself, might constitute the high point of the Sunday eucharistic liturgy for many participants. One of the speakers, John Baldovin, surmised that the sense of togetherness which was being sought in the liturgy was precisely what was lacking in other dimensions of daily life. He was perturbed by this hypothesis and worried that such a tendency would lead to a diminishment in appreciation of the eucharist. He decided to compare the findings of the survey with the five aspects of the eucharist acknowledged in the 'Baptism, Eucharist and Ministry Document' (Lima) of the World Council of Churches. These were: Thanksgiving to the Father, Anamnesis or Memorial of Christ, Invocation of the Holy Spirit, Communion of the faithful and Meal of the kingdom. He found that only one of these, 'Communion of the faithful', predominated in the responses of the survey. In itself, this predominance of a single category should not be a cause of concern since the interpretation of eucharist as sacrifice was so dominant in Roman Catholicism that it displaced all others for well over 1,000 years. In fact there are those who would welcome this development and see it as highlighting an aspect of the eucharist which was sadly neglected in the practice of the past. Yet it is a very disquieting finding for it raises the question: What is happening to the other vital, awesome and challenging dimensions of the eucharist? Is there a demand here that liturgy be merely a comfortable extension of the self? These questions become even more disturbing when mention of the integral link between the celebration of eucharist and the doing of justice is notably absent from the survey.

Before leaving the survey, it should be noted that in it the proclamation of the word was heard and remembered because of
the personality of the readers rather than for its content. Many
people remembered that 'the lector read well' but remembered
nothing of what was read! Furthermore, although the *General
Instruction on the Roman Missal* insists that the eucharistic prayer
is the 'centre and high point of the celebration' (54) most of those
surveyed found it to be the dullest part of the eucharistic liturgy,
though a few confessed that they prayed it by heart with the
priest. Finally, there was near universal dissatisfaction with the
homily.

Of course we might want to say, 'Well that's the US, it's not us',
or argue that the results are predictable from even a cursory
reading of *Habits of the Heart* (Bellah et al) or *The Culture of
Narcissism* (C. Lasch). Certainly there are substantial differences
between what is represented in the survey and what takes place
at the average Sunday eucharist in Ireland. There is little danger
yet that our contrived and self-conscious gestures at the sign of
peace will be taken as the high-point of the liturgy! However,
those of us who stand at the back or the front of the Sunday
assembly and wonder why the congregation returns week after
week, will find enough similarities in that survey to give pause
for thought. How different would the comments about the
proclamation of the word, about the homily, about the eucharistic
prayer, be after most of our Sunday Masses? And what answer
do we have to the harder questions: Is the 82% who come to
weekly Mass more just, more loving, more committed to the
poor, the marginalised, the dispossessed, the unemployed? Are
they more concerned about the contradictions between what is
done around the Lord's table and so much of what is happening
in the local and global contexts? How many wonder how we can
'take bread and wine' in a world of injustice and hunger? 'How
many Catholics, when they receive the eucharist, experience a
demand to overcome the divisions between Catholics and
Protestants and between Nationalists and Unionists? How
many Catholics in the Republic see the question of Articles 2 and
3 of the constitution as an issue to be considered in the light of
the gospel-demand to make peace?' (*Solidarity: The missing Link
in Irish Society*, Jesuit Centre for Faith and Justice)

Faith and culture

Culture may be defined as 'a system of symbols, rites, images, beliefs, values, ideas and ethical norms that a people holds in common and that gives a populace a way of living in the world'. (D. Power, *The Eucharistic Mystery*, Gill and Macmillan, 1992). Reviewed in the light of this definition, it becomes obvious that much of the preceding material has in fact been concerned with the links between culture and liturgy. Questions about these links must first be situated within the wider context of the relationship between faith and culture that has become a central issue since the Second Vatican Council. This is not to suggest that the relationship began in the 1960s, but the publication of the *Pastoral Constitution on the Church in the Modern World* in 1965 in particular, provided an exciting new charter for on-going dialogue. That charter has been confirmed and extended by successive Popes: 'Adaptation of the gospel to culture is not only legitimate but desirable' (Paul VI) … 'The synthesis between faith and culture is not just a demand of culture but also of faith' (John Paul II). Both Popes saw the relationship between gospel and culture as absolutely pivotal if evangelisation were to succeed. Paul VI saw the split between them as 'the drama of our time'; John Paul II considers the 'church's dialogue with the cultures of our time to be a vital area, one in which the destiny of the world at the end of the century is at stake'. The extraordinary Synod of Bishops in 1985 considered the question of inculturation (a word first used by John Paul II in 1979) and pointed out that the church 'takes up whatever it finds positive in all cultures'. It went on: 'Inculturation, however, is different from a mere external adaptation, as it signifies an interior transformation of authentic cultural values through their integration into Christianity and the rooting of Christianity in various human cultures'.

Obviously the authors of these texts had in mind something quite different from the imposition of the Christian faith on particular cultures and something much more profound than a mere translation of the gospel into the languages of various peoples. Rather, they were boldly proposing a vital and vibrant interaction that would be reciprocal and transformative for both actants, while each would retain their specific identity. Yet despite the sanction for this dialogue with culture offered by council, synod and Popes, the conversation has not been easy-going, even at a theoretical level. The very variety of words used to name the process (many of them transposed from anthropology) and the divergent meanings given to them, tell their own story: incarnation, indiginisation, adaptation, contextualisation, acculturation and inculturation. There is now substantial agreement that 'inculturation' is the most suitable term to describe the encounter. This term is often contrasted with another, 'acculturation', which is closer to the 'external adaptation' mentioned above by the synod. The image here is of two strangers being introduced. It speaks of a polite, tolerant, respectful, juxtaposition of two cultures that does not reach beyond the level of external interaction. Inculturation may truly be the better term but the reciprocal interaction of gospel and culture and the processes of critical assimilation and creative transformation which it implies, have proved very difficult to carry through in practice. In any serious contact between gospel and culture, a critical and cautious approach is understandable from the side of church leadership, for it is difficult to balance the hopes for the enrichment that can come from culture against the fear of impoverishment or dilution of the gospel. And it must honestly be admitted that many cultural realities may be alien or even downright inimical to the gospel. But at times that difficulty and fear seem to have led to paralysis. As a consequence, culture's revelatory potential, while being acknowledged officially at a theoretical level, has often been denied at a practical level.

Liturgy and culture
When we move to the more specific question of the relationship between liturgy and culture, we might expect that the dialogue would be more fulsome and the interaction more fruitful. After all, our liturgy has always been culturally conditioned and liturgical history offers many examples of successful inculturation which could serve as precedent for what needs to be done today. The Christian eucharist itself is a study of the creative assimilation of Jewish prayer-forms and their transformation within a new ritual matrix. Although the Christian stance towards the Greco-Roman world was largely counter-cultural and its words of address polemical, we still find elements of pagan birthing rituals being incorporated into third-century rites of Christian initiation. Later the culturally-conditioned patterns of thinking

and praying, and the oratorical style of the Roman world in the fourth to the seventh centuries, can be heard in 'the noble simplicity and sobriety' that are said to characterise the 'classical' Roman liturgy. That splendid achievement had itself to be radically revamped in the eighth century to take account of the very different sensibilities of worshippers within the Franco-Roman empire. In the tenth century that unique liturgical creation, with its characteristic vigour and expressivity, was in turn incorporated into the Roman tradition and brought with it the rituals of the Great Week and in particular the Easter vigil.

The *Constitution on the Sacred Liturgy* sought to 'undertake with great care a general restoration of the liturgy itself'. (SC 21) That was possible because 'the liturgy is made up of unchangeable elements divinely instituted, and of elements subject to change. The latter not only may be changed, but ought to be changed ... if they have suffered from the intrusion of anything out of harmony with the inner nature of the liturgy and have become less suitable'. (ibid) Furthermore it opened the door to the possibility of liturgical pluralism: 'The church does not wish to impose a rigid uniformity in matters which do not involve the faith or the good of the whole community, rather does she respect and foster the qualities and talents of the various races and nations.'(37) Finally it took a more radical step when it recognised that ecclesiastical authorities were competent not only to institute adaptation regarding sacraments and sacramentals but even 'to admit into divine worship' appropriate elements 'from the traditions and cultures of individual peoples'.(40) The 1969 *Instruction on the Translation of Liturgical Texts* openly declared that 'texts translated from another language are clearly not sufficient for the celebration of a fully renewed liturgy. The creation of new texts will be necessary'.

It is understandable that, after the council, much of the energy of liturgists went into revising and translating and publishing the typical editions of the liturgical books, and the amazing output of material from 1968 to 1974 bears witness to their dedication. Yet when we re-read the foregoing quotations and then scan that material and recall its 'reception' at local level, it is difficult to avoid the impression that there is something seriously amiss. Yes, the textual and ritual revisions were complete by the mid 1970s, but in both their preparation and implementation the de-

sire for standardisation and globalisation seemed to be para-
mount. The directives above concerning inculturation appeared
to be forgotten, and indeed no attempt has ever been made to
acknowledge the cultural conditioning and cultural patterns
already implicit in the typical editions themselves and their
sources! So, apart from the Zaire Rite (and it experienced difficulty in gaining official approval) and one or two instances in
India, the process of liturgical adaptation experienced by most
Roman Catholics has been largely one of *acculturation* rather
than *inculturation*. We have translations from 'the foreign language' of the typical editions, but even where these translations
have striven for dynamic rather than literal equivalence, the criteria seem to have been ultimately linguistic rather than cultural
(e.g. texts for *the English-speaking world* as if it were culturally
homogeneous!). These translations have then been proclaimed
to people whose own diverse cultural patterns (their typical
modes of thinking and communicating, and ritualising their values and traditions) have been largely ignored. (See A. Chup-
ungco, *Liturgical Inculturation*, Pueblo, 1992).

In the early days of post-conciliar reform, the texts of the new
typical editions were appearing with great frequency and we
were so mesmerised by the strangeness of hearing them speak to
us in a language that *seemed* to be our own, that we overlooked
their shortcomings. We probably knew intuitively what may
now be stated technically: that acculturation is the necessary
first step in the process of inculturation. Accordingly, we had
great hopes for what would be achieved as further steps led to
deeper acquaintance. As a next step, it would have been necessary to acknowledge that liturgy is always the public worship of
a particular assembly who are members of a particular ethnic
group and a particular culture, and then work with the implications of that reality. But sadly, that step and the necessary further steps did not follow.

So when some people today listen to the solemn, hieratic, but
dry and unemotive words of the text of a Sunday liturgy, they
may well ask: what acknowledgement is there in this of the
poetic prayer-forms of our own Irish tradition? Or they may listen to the prayers of even the much improved *Order of Christian
Funerals* and ask: Is this the best that can be offered out of 'the
genius and tradition' (SC 37) of a people that believes passion-

ately in communion with the living dead and that gave the world the institution known as the Irish wake?

When what was once acceptable and even taken-for-granted begins to jar, or at times embarrass, worshippers may conclude that they are listening to a foreign production, dubbed in a universalised English voice-over, but spoken with a local accent. If this is true, it is no wonder that wholehearted participation in the liturgy and a dynamic relationship between life and liturgy seem so difficult to achieve. It is no wonder either that expectations in regard to the homily are so high – in those circumstances, it must of necessity become a crucial (for some, the only) instrument for achieving appropriate translation and cultural mediation. It is no wonder either that disappointment is so keenly felt when it fails in its maieutic role.

The relationship between culture and liturgy is the central question that needs to be faced in on-going renewal. So far, the concern has been mainly with what liturgy may bring to culture. While this is important, it fails to acknowledge what culture, which powerfully influences every aspect of our lives, has been bringing to bear on those who celebrate liturgy.

Religiosity of the people
Closely allied to the discussion on liturgy and culture is the question of popular religiosity. In the constitution on the liturgy there is only one reference to one form of popular religiosity, namely popular devotions (*pia exercitia*). That reference (SC 13) highly recommends popular devotions that 'conform to the laws and norms of the church' but suggests that they be brought into closer harmony with the liturgy. It ends with a strong reminder that 'the liturgy by its nature is far superior' to any such devotions. After the council, the focus of interest and energy was the renewed liturgy itself and it was believed that when it was properly implemented and appreciated, it would deliver what had previously been sought in popular devotions. People, who as spectators at the sacred drama of the silent Latin Mass had grown accustomed to substituting devotions for active participation, were expected now to become active participants in the renewed liturgy. The sudden transition from praying *at Mass* to *praying the Mass* was difficult for many and impossible for some.

During those post-conciliar years, official support for many popular devotions declined. They were regarded by some people as excessively individualistic or unscriptural (or just plain old-fashioned) and some devotions were suppressed. Certain critics of liturgical renewal believed that it had by-passed people's piety, deprived them of what they possessed in order to give them the ideal. This created an affective vacuum in many people's lives which they have tried to fill in various ways since. This situation has never been adequately addressed, so today devotions and liturgy continue, uncomfortably, side by side.

The 70s saw a certain revival of some traditional practices but also the beginnings of a theological reappraisal of the relationship between popular religiosity and liturgy. It became clear that the distinction between 'public and private prayer' and between 'liturgical and non-liturgical prayer', which had been rigorously maintained, needed rethinking and that the definition of liturgy which underpinned them needed to be broadened. It began to be recognised that prayer, whether official or popular is *leiton ergon*, it is 'a work of the people', it is *worship*, that is, it is about people shaping what is of ultimate worth to them. The common and most important factor in both modes of prayer is quite simply the same: people at prayer. The difference lies in the choice of different prayer-forms to articulate their desire for communion with the holy.

Theological reflection too, while acknowledging the ambivalence of some devotions and the possibility of admixture with superstition, enabled people to understand that the varied expressions of popular religiosity were themselves products of inculturation (even if in some cases culture seemed to have the edge on the gospel!) The study of liturgical history helped people to realise that some of what we regard as high-points of our liturgical cycle, even significant rituals of Holy Week, in fact grew out of popular practices (see above). It also clarified the fact that the general Roman Catholic understanding of the Mass was shaped much more by eucharistic devotion than by sacramental theology.

Pastoral experience also made it clear that many people did not experience the renewed liturgy as speaking to their daily lives in a transforming way. The liturgy, even in the vernacular, still seemed remote and otherworldly to many participants, failing to address their yearnings and fears, their pain and failure and loneliness. It became clearer too that there could frequently be a tension between what the renewal intended and what people believed they wanted. The renewed rites of, for example, baptism and marriage, might stress that they were ecclesial celebrations of the local Christian community, yet in practice the 'community' might be confined to family and friends and the rituals of the 'real' celebration might well take place elsewhere.

That ongoing reappraisal reached something of a climax in the Puebla Document (1979) which declared that there should be 'a mutual and enriching exchange between the liturgy and popular devotion'.

Those who write about expressions of popular religiosity mention characteristics such as familiarity with the holy, the use of images, self-involvement, festivity, affectivity, exuberance, spontaneity, and concrete, intimate and repetitive language. These characteristics are often contrasted with the sober, concise, elegant, rational formality of the Roman liturgy. They further note that in most forms of popular religiosity participants are much more actively engaged than in the official liturgy; that the self-as-body is much more holistically involved; that as pray-ers they have a greater sense of being in control of the process and a greater awareness of their own position within it as powerful petitioners and intercessors, confidants of Mary and the saints. It is because of this contrast between what have been called 'prayer of the head and prayer of the heart' that the Puebla Document can look forward to 'a mutual and enriching exchange' between them. Worship should involve the response of the whole person – emotions, intellect and will.

This does not mean that we may 'baptise' everything or that we should simply encourage the unquestioning rehabilitation of traditional devotions in a vastly changed context (as has been happening in some places). Nor does it mean that we should refrain from introducing what David Power aptly called 'prophetic dissonance' into those manifestations of popular religiosity still in vogue, in order to realign them (where necessary) with gospel priorities. Neither does it mean condoning attempts to merge the eucharist and devotional practices contrary to the warnings of Pope Paul VI against such 'hybrid celebrations'. (*Marialis Cultus* 31) And finally it does not mean that we can deny the difficulty of dealing with manifestations of popular religiosity or ignore the current debates about its meaning and methodology.

It does mean, however, examining the phenomenon of the enthusiastic participation of so many Irish people in novenas, pilgrim-
ages and processions (and even their response to so-called moving statues!). It means trying to understand why some people
who otherwise do not attend 'either Mass or meeting' join the
Christian community for the Lenten Ashes, Good Friday
Veneration of the Cross and the Christmas Vigil. Then, in the
light of the insights gained, it would be necessary to explore
how the powerful attraction that expressions of popular religiosity have for many people might be harnessed so as to enhance
our liturgical celebrations. What would be sought would be at
the level of inspiration and nurturing genius rather than in the
detail of forms. This would be done so that the 'creative dynamism' (Puebla 465) of popular religiosity might be married to the
imaginative possibilities of the renewed liturgy.

Spirituality

The liturgy constitution did not merely institute ritual reform –
it sought above all to bring about the renewal of Christian life
and spirituality. The years since the council have seen a bur-
geoning interest in spirituality. The relatedness of spirituality,
liturgy and culture has been receiving attention in recent writings by some theologians and religious educators. I will not attempt to summarise that literature but will instead refer to the
works of two representative authors. Writing about catechesis
and spirituality, Michael Warren[2] takes issue with those who
tend to equate spirituality with prayer or with a narrow concept
of contemplation. He insists that, 'In a very real sense one cannot
not have a spirituality. Every human person as an embodied
spirit is a being whose spirit has been shaped by commitments,
choices, hopes, uses of time and so forth. The question can never
be, 'will we have a spirituality?' but, rather, 'what kind of spirituality will we have?'' This is what some authors call the philo-
sophical meaning of spirituality and what Warren himself calls
'lower-case' spirituality. By contrast he sees 'upper-case' spirituality as involving 'an active disciplined search for God' and the
description of that search which he finds most helpful is: 'A systematic way of attending to the presence of God.' He continues
'… it is a system, a way and not just a way in the mind.' It is
worth recalling again the extract quoted in chapter three: 'A

spirituality is a way of walking, a particular way of being in the world. It is entirely possible to have two conflicting spiritual- ities, a verbal or a notional one, which we might claim guides our lives, and the lived one, which is the actual one. The first is an illusory spirituality, which is named and not lived, but which belies the actual spirituality, which is lived but not always named. Thus it is possible to claim in verbal declaration that we have a Christian spirituality, whereas the actual way we struct- ure our lives down to our simplest decisions is not based on the gospels at all. Quite simply a spirituality that does not affect life- structure is not the actual spirituality.'

If this is true, what happens when we gather for liturgical cele- brations? How could a fragile and vulnerable liturgy overcome that conflict between our notional and actual spiritualities?

Other authorities, drawing on the researches of social analysts and historians of religion, have tried to shed light on this painful disjunction between what we proclaim in prayer and what we live in daily life. Those researches suggest that, as a consequence of the growing stress on the autonomy of the individual and the subjective, there has been a loss of confidence in political, social and cultural institutions. Psychology and psychiatry have tended to fill that void. The idioms of therapy have invaded the social, cultural and educational realms and we are 'held together' by the patterns of production and consumption rather than by a common vision. They suggest further that such changed struct- ures, priorities and values could put pressure on religious peo- ple to relegate matters of ultimate concern to the private realm and to locate the holy in the depths of the self or the intimate group rather than in publically shared rituals. It would, they believe, demand strength and discerning wisdom on the part of religious people to resist such pressure. Some interchange be- tween our world and our spiritualities is of course inevitable and necessary, for all models of spiritualities are the outcome of inculturation of the gospel in the lived experience of Christians in differing cultural and historical contexts. The authors[3] I have read believe that by our refusal to face (or at times even acknow- ledge) the cultural question, we have not only lost an opportunity for enrichment but have given free rein to all manner of negative influences which have been shaping our attitudes, values and language. What alarms them most is the extent to which the negative dynamics of our culture have been absorbed imperceptibly by casual contagion into our 'lower-case' or lived spiritualities. (Has it been the case that our dominant spirituality, the Journey Inwards, with its conviction about privileged modes of access to the holy, was most susceptible to this kind of cultural pressure?) One of the authors, Peter Fink, says that in the present context, where spirituality tends to be spoken of in terms of personal growth and fulfilment, recognition and affirmation, he is concerned that it ... 'can too easily be read through the lens of a psychological paradigm and become quasi-therapy rather than true spiritual growth'. He continues:

> I weep when the Enneagram or the Myers-Briggs analysis replaces the almost erotic intimacy with Christ described by John of the Cross in his 'Dark night of the soul', or the stunning challenge to discipleship and companionship presented in some of the great Ignatian meditations on the mystery of Christ.The psychological tools are fun and even helpful, but they create a fascination with oneself and, in the end, leave us alone with that fascination. I grow very sad when the paradoxical wisdom of our heroines and heroes is replaced by the strategies and stages of the psychological paradigm. A language that was once very large and awesomely beautiful has been transformed into a language that is very self-centered and very small.

The conclusion from all of this is not only that negative aspects of our culture have infiltrated our spiritualities in destructive ways, but that paradoxically our very spiritualities may be preventing us from hearing and responding to the challenge of the liturgy. If there is truth in this, then we need to strive to recover the vision offered by the liturgy *Constitution*: 'It is through the liturgy especially that the faithful are enabled to express in their lives, and manifest to others, the mystery of Christ and the real nature of the Church.' (SC 2) We need desperately to be reminded (and liturgy is anamnesis) of what our culture would have us forget: That we gather as a priestly, prophetic and diaconal people to share in this 'action of Christ the priest and of his Body which is the church'. (SC 7); that the liturgy's vision is about the kingdom; that its concern is the worship of God and the transformation of humanity; that we need its mediation and its motivation so that we may be weaned away from being self-concerned and self-centred.

Leadership

Fifteen years after the promulgation of the liturgy *Constitution*, an article appeared in *The Furrow* entitled 'Liturgy after Vatican II', with the intriguing sub-title 'Harmful Vacillation or Reconciling Genius?'[4] In it the author sought to charter the tensions and inconsistencies which appeared in the progressive redactions of certain key texts of the liturgical renewal. He pointed out that '... the tone, the terminology and even the underlying theology has varied from document to document and at times within the same document.' In the intervening fifteen years, many more documents have appeared and, no doubt, he would ask the same question about some of them. Two documents in particular, one granting permission to celebrate the Latin Tridentine Mass (1984), the other introducing *The Order for Sunday celebration in the absence of a priest* (1989), continue to perplex many people as they attempt to reconcile them with the *Constitution*'s charter for liturgical renewal.

The tensions and inconsistencies are not confined to official documents. The Holy See may keep a watchful eye on the liturgy; it may be diligent in clarifying disputed questions and warning against abuses; episcopal conferences may insist on ritual norms; they may issue directives and promote liturgical programmes; but in the end of the day, the decisions, the choices, the selections and the judgements made at the level of the local assembly will have the most powerful influence on the liturgy as it is celebrated. This highlights the extraordinary and frightening power that the local priest has over the celebration of the liturgy. That power may be exercised through valid judgement, selection and decision concerning the range of options available, but also through filtering or even suppressing some of those options. The consequences of this exercise of power can be seen in the substantial differences in the celebration of Sunday eucharist between parish and parish, and even within the same parish. No doubt differing ecclesiologies and differing models of grace and salvation have their influence, but it is very difficult to understand what criteria are being used as a basis for some of these judgements. Priests, who may be utterly meticulous in observing the minutiae of some norms and regulations, may blithely ignore other directives that affect the very core of the celebration.

To take one very glaring example: The *General Instruction of the Roman Missal* says, 'The nature of the sign demands that the material for the eucharistic celebration appear as actual food. The eucharistic bread, even though unleavened and traditional in form, should therefore be made in such a way that the priest can break it and distribute the parts to at least some of the faithful ... The gesture of the breaking of the bread, as the eucharist was called in apostolic times, will more clearly show the eucharist as a sign of unity and charity, since the one bread is being distributed among the members of one family.' (GIRM 283) It would be expected that this demand – that what is 'taken' at the eucharist should appear as actual food, which is so fundamental and so symbolically significant – would be met by universal compliance. Instead we have used the concession found in that same paragraph, 'When the number of communicants is large or other pastoral needs require it, small hosts may be used,' to universally ignore that demand. We appear to read it as if it meant that small hosts (white or brown!) do not have to look like real food and that 'may' really means 'must'!

Women and liturgy

This topic has been left until last, not because it is of least importance, but because it can only be addressed adequately by women. Here I wish only to mention three random points which I trust will be acceptable, despite my 'outsider' status! The tensions and inconsistencies mentioned in the previous section are found in abundance in relation to the present topic. A recurring preoccupation is that of finding a 'suitable place' for women ministers within the liturgical assembly. The *Third General Instruction on the Proper Implementation of the Liturgical Constitution* (1970) declared that '... in conformity with norms traditional in the church, women (single, married, religious), whether in churches, homes, convents, schools or institutions for women, are barred from serving at the altar.' They could, however, announce the intentions in the general intercessions, sing and play musical instruments, read a commentary, organise processions and even take up the collection. Women were allowed to proclaim the readings, except the gospel, and if they did, conferences of bishops were to 'give specific directions on the place best suited for women to read the word of God in the liturgical assembly.' The

1975 edition of the GIRM directed that 'Lay men ... may perform all the functions below those reserved to deacons. At the discretion of the rector of the church, women may be appointed to ministries outside the sanctuary. The conference of bishops may permit qualified women to proclaim the readings before the gospel ... (they) may also more precisely designate a suitable place for women to proclaim the word of God in the liturgical assembly.'

Today women freely enter the sanctuary to proclaim the word of God, to arrange the table of the eucharist, to act as ministers of communion, and to bring the sacrament to the housebound. In some parts of the world, where no ordained minister is available, women, by episcopal mandate, proclaim the gospel, deliver the homily and lead the service of communion in the reserved sacrament. Yet the earlier stipulations remain 'on the books' and may at times be invoked with disconcerting consequences.

Secondly, a question. In the 820 pages of text in the American survey mentioned earlier, there were only two references to women and liturgy – one to inclusive language, the other to discriminatory treatment of a woman by a male usher. Are we to assume that all the other women interviewed had no difficulties with the liturgy as celebrated, or could it be that those who had, no longer participated?

Finally, it seems that in relation to women, the church as institution, down through the centuries, has listened to the mores of the dominant culture rather than to the culturally subversive, credal formula of Galatians 3:24-29. Now that the cultural situation is changing so dramatically, it presents a great challenge to the church to recover the implications of that text. In relation to the prayer of the church, a beginning might be made by publicly acknowledging the extent to which the flourishing of the diaconal and the devotional owes a special debt of gratitude to women. This, in turn, should lead to repentance for the gender discrimination of the past and a search by women and men together for more diverse ways of ministry.

Conclusion
Thirty years after the promulgation of the *Constitution on the Sacred Liturgy*, some commentators are suggesting that we are

just now in a good position to re-read it and begin to renew the liturgy – doing it right this time! Whatever about that, there is certainly plenty of work still to be done. The constant refrain of this chapter has been the need to face the fraught question of the relationship between culture and liturgy. Yet it must be said that that question cannot be faced 'head-on' because the ultimate problem is not culture in itself, but rather where we as worshippers stand in relation to culture. Facing that problem would mean examining the ground on which we stand – especially our claims to follow the way of Jesus of Nazareth, our models of grace and salvation, and our ultimate foundational roots in ritual, symbol and narrative. That should keep us busy for at least another decade!

Notes

1. Smulders, P., *The Fathers on Christology*, St Norbert's Abbey Press, 1968, 1.

2. *Faith, Culture and the Worshipping Community*, The Pastoral Press, 1993, 71-76.

3. Note the remarkable convergence between the first three contributors to E. Bernstein (ed): *Liturgy and Spirituality in Context*, The Liturgical Press, 1990.

4. McKenna, John, 'Liturgy after Vatican II', *The Furrow*, March 1979, 154-167.

Part II

Interlude

When we scan the foregoing reviews of the achievements and shortcomings of liturgical renewal to date, does any sense of the direction to be taken for the future emerge? Some people may be inclined to respond by saying that we should 'leave very well alone' and be content with the familiarity of what has been achieved. Others may say that many of the issues critiqued in those chapters should be addressed immediately and that the more intractable problems, such as the relationship between liturgy and culture, should become top priorities in the years ahead. I could certainly agree with the latter proposal, yet niggling doubts remain.

Such measures would, no doubt, overcome many of the present anomalies and ensure that we enjoyed richer and more congruent liturgies. But, would they come to grips with the even deeper problems facing us? I find it difficult to say clearly what these problems are, and even more difficult to divine their causes. My attempts to articulate them to myself generally take the form of paradox or hypothesis. Is it the case that focusing too narrowly on the liturgy in itself, without taking other critical factors into account, has given rise to our most basic problems? Are the real problems with liturgy to be located in people and their spiritualities, rather than in the liturgy itself? Do these problems exist because we have been asking, simultaneously, too much and too little from the liturgy during the years since the council?

Too little
First of all, as is obvious from the previous chapters, I believe that we have tended to rest satisfied with liturgies that were less than adequate or were even inconsistent with the foundational vision of the reform itself. But beyond this complacency, another more disturbing dynamic has been at work. Since Vatican II, we have been asked to come to accept, and live by, more adequate

and more coherent images of the divine-human relationship, of Christ, of the church, of the assembly, and to bring these enrichments to the celebration of the liturgy. However, many of us seem to have resisted that invitation, and have preferred instead the familiarity of older models which are at variance with what is presented in the renewed liturgy. In relation to the eucharist, for example, we may yield, consciously or unconsciously, to the temptation to filter and diminish what the eucharistic liturgy seeks to communicate to us about God, Christ, the church, salvation, and ourselves, so that it coincides with what *we* think the eucharist *should* be. Instead of being conformed to the eucharist, we are conforming it to ourselves, we are re-forming it in our image and likeness.

If this is so, then we are suffering from a self-imposed impoverishment which is in danger of neutralising the powerful mediations of liturgy in ritual, symbol, and narrative. It seems that we recognise, intuitively, the subversive character of liturgical anamnesis, and then seek ways of controlling it. Of course I believe in the transforming power of grace, and I believe that exposure to ritual, which affects us at all levels of our being, can break through our shell of resistance. But I also believe that resisting that in which we are taking part is neither an appropriate nor a fruitful mode of presence. I do not think that we should expect the liturgy to achieve its goal in spite of us.

Too much
When I speak of 'expecting too much of the liturgy', let me say straight away that we should aspire to having the best possible liturgies. I am thinking here, rather, of the writings of some liturgists which tend to concentrate on idealised, theoretically possible celebrations of the liturgy. Sometimes they seem to forget that liturgical texts and interpretations are only words on a page until they are enacted by the participants. Once the worshipping participants are included, we must deal with an incredible variety and pluriformity of convictions and responses.

I also have in mind the more important issue of the huge expectations which participants can have of liturgical celebrations. Sometimes we talk about the celebration of the eucharist, for example, as if we could expect from it what, in fact, could only be found in the fullness of a converted life, as if what takes place during a celebration could stand in lieu of the rest of our lives.

The eucharist challenges us to live differently, to be converted, to be committed to discipleship, but it cannot do these things for us. What is proposed ritually to us in the eucharist, must be actively incarnated in our lives. Because we are aware of the powerful symbolic character of the eucharist, and all liturgy, we frequently seem to forget how fragile and vulnerable it is. We forget the disturbing lessons of history, which make clear the extent to which the meaning of the eucharist was diminished and distorted by social, cultural, theological and personal factors. We forget, above all, how utterly dependent it is on our consistent embodiment of its mystery.

Perhaps another way of expressing this is to recall that, in the last thirty years, we have tended to work on the basic assumption that renewal of the liturgy would lead to renewal of life. We seem to recognise more clearly now the dialectical relationship that exists between these two forms of renewal. We realise that our praise must prove itself to be authentic, must be veri-fied or falsified, in our praxis; and our praxis is inspired by, and is taken up into a higher harmony, in our praise.

A contribution

If the ultimate problems that we associate with liturgy are to be located at these levels, then what is called for, first and foremost, is ongoing conversion, and committed and consistent discipleship. Out of that transformation we would celebrate liturgy very differently! This would demand a mystagogy of praxis and praise, rather than a theoretical, liturgical or theological approach. However, I believe that a liturgical theology which endeavoured to rediscover the foundations for praxis and praise, could make a modest contribution to that process. I hope that the rest of this book might be seen as one such modest contribution.

In chapter five we will seek to recover the sense of awe, wonder and fascination before the graciousness of God, from which praxis and praise spring in the Jewish and Christian traditions. Chapter six explores nine models which have been used, down through the centuries, to communicate certain convictions about salvation in Jesus Christ. It must be admitted that some of them have had disastrous consequences for Christian praxis and praise. In chapter seven we are invited to attend to the implications of the model of liberation, which is judged by church leaders to be appropriate and necessary for our times. Readers are invited to identify their own dominant model and, should they judge it to be less than adequate and satisfying, to replace it by another which is more consistent with the scriptural tradition. Chapter eight begins with a review of the sacramental theology in vogue prior to Vatican II and hints at some of the theological developments since then. In particular, it outlines an approach to ritual, symbol and narrative, and points to their transformative effects within Israel. Finally, chapter nine looks at the message and ministry, death and new life of Jesus Christ as a paradigm of God's grace and salvation, and the foundation for our praxis and praise.

As the image of the wheel, which is used in chapter eight, suggests, the concern of these chapters is with the connectedness and mutual enrichment of foundational themes. Progress may, at times, be in a cyclical rather than a strictly linear mode.

CHAPTER 5

Grace and salvation
in the scriptures

God must be allowed to surprise us
(Patrick Kavanagh)

Christians have always believed that liturgy and sacraments existed only because of God's grace and salvation. But there have been extraordinary variations in the way in which they have interpreted the relationship between them. These have ranged from spontaneous, heartfelt response to the experience of God's love and mercy, to a quasi-magical attempt to manipulate God's power. In this chapter, we will seek to uncover the ultimate basis for the praise and thanksgiving of liturgy in the experience of God's gracious salvation, recorded for us in the scriptures.[1] Particular attention will be given to a set of words in the First Testament, which seeks to name the most significant dimensions of the relationship between God and Israel. The words 'grace' and 'salvation' may be distinguished, but God's salvation *is* grace, God's grace *is* salvation. Next, we will attend, briefly, to the life and ministry of Jesus of Nazareth, God's gracious and definitive salvation incarnate. Finally, we will study the Pauline and Johannine understanding of grace.

Reference is made to the Hebrew and Greek words, not as an exercise in pedantry, but because of the difficulty of translation. Introducing the Greek translation of the book of Sirach, the author's grandson begs indulgence of the reader for 'despite our diligent labour in translating, we may seem to have rendered some phrases imperfectly. For what was originally expressed in Hebrew does not have exactly the same sense when translated into another language'.

The conviction guiding this chapter is that what is named as grace in experience is what is proclaimed in liturgy.

1. The First Testament

Hanan

The foundational images in the Hebrew verb *hanan* are: bending low, inclining towards, focusing attention on something or someone. With reference to human relations, it means being gracious towards, showing favour to, having mercy on someone. This benevolence does not remain at the level of inner disposition but embodies itself in transforming action on behalf of the other. The recipient of this gracious favour is always seen to stand in a position of structural inferiority to the benefactor, yet the motive for the action is never one of condescension. It springs from love alone, so *hanan* denotes the unmerited, heartfelt initiative of one who is richly endowed turning towards another who has nothing or is in a state of critical need. What mobilises this initiative is not some positive quality in the recipient; rather the undeserved gracious action comes from the benefactor alone. It is inspired only by loving kindness and it is always undertaken in sovereign freedom.

The quality of *hanan* is manifested, characteristically, in having mercy on the poor, pardoning offenders, sparing the defenceless, granting unconditional forgiveness, being gentle with the vulnerable and delivering the distressed from their anguish. The rich register of meanings of this word in the field of human relationships no doubt recommended its use as an apt metaphor to gain insight into the relationship between Israel and her God. Israel believed that she had been freely chosen as Yahweh's special possession only because of the sheer graciousness of God's love. 'From among the families of the earth I have known only you'. (Amos 3:2) There was nothing in her to merit such an extraordinary initiative. (Ez 16, Hos 11). She has no claim or title to God's providential care for her, no warrant for God's passionate involvement in her history and destiny. Everything she was and had was pure gift from the One who 'always listened to the cry of her distress' and 'loved her with an everlasting love'. *Hanan* is used about sixty times in the Hebrew bible and in more than forty instances God is its subject. In some passages it is placed on the lips of Yahweh as a word of virtual self-definition. 'I will make all my goodness pass before you and will proclaim before you my name, The Lord, and I will be gracious to whom I will be gracious and will show mercy on whom I will show mercy.'

And again, 'The Lord, a God merciful and gracious, slow to anger and abounding in steadfast love and faithfulness, keeping steadfast love for a thousand generations'. (Ex 34:7) Godself is revealed as free and sovereign graciousness.

The term is found with notable frequency in the psalms where, in situations characterised by oppression, poverty, misery, sinfulness and the threat of death, the psalmists implore God's favour. They can pray with absolute assurance that God will be gracious to them because their God cares in a special way for the weak and the lost. Understandably, 'Be gracious to me' is a recurring refrain in many psalms. Again it must be made clear that God is not understood as responding to some positive attributes or dispositions of the petitioner, but rather is acting in accordance with the characteristic of Godself – graciousness. So it is *because* they are weak, lost and defenceless that they are especially loved by this gracious, merciful God of *hanan*.

Yet we must remember that their petitions (like the entire life of Israel) are prayed out of situations of dialogue, which alerts us to the fact that the innate inequality of the relationship is tempered by a constant invitation to mutuality (see Ex 33:12-23). Again her insight into the transforming power of interpersonal love would have been significant here. The creative love of God could not be without effect in her life and, transformed by it, could she not make bold to give herself in love to the source from which she came?

Hen
We might expect that the noun *hen*, which is derived from the verb *hanan*, would mean gift or favour conferred on someone. But instead we find that it has broken free of the dominant meaning of its verbal roots and its connotations are significantly different. The focus is no longer on the gracious giver who confers a favour, but rather on a characteristic or disposition of someone which enables them to win favour from someone else (always structurally a superior). Qualities such as beauty, charm, elegance, gracefulness, may arouse that favourable response, so that their possessor is said 'to find favour in the eyes of someone' – as the typical phrase has it. From a religious perspective it might be possible to argue that such qualities derive ultimately from 'God's better beauty, grace' (Hopkins) but this misses the point. God as source is quite simply not included in the range of

meaning of the word *hen*. Because of this semantic shift, *hen* cannot serve as the correlative noun of *hanan*. Instead its place is taken by the word *hesed*.

Hesed

The provenance of the word *hesed* is that of reciprocal relations in a group, with special emphasis on what promotes bonding and group solidarity. However it would be a serious misunderstanding of *hesed* to limit it to a concern with status, roles, rights and obligations. By contrast, it communicates a sense of intimacy, spontaneity, prodigality and exuberance in human relationships. *Hesed* is the generous impulse, the surprising beneficence towards another, the devoted dedication to their life and wellbeing. The spotlight is on the one who initiates *hesed* but, more forcefully than *hanan*, it seeks a response of *hesed* and encourages mutuality. Because *hesed* speaks about what is best and most alluring in human affairs, it was fitting that it be used analogically to speak of the relationship between Israel and God. The paradigmatic events of the Exodus from Egypt, the establishment of the Covenant and the entry into the promised land, convinced Israel that God cared for her in an extraordinary way. Although she had been created as a people out of the nothingness of slavery by the wondrous and prodigal love of God, yet that same God was wooing her constantly and seeking to coax her back to the pristine excitement of first love.

This extravagant and passionate love, which was 'beyond saying sweet, past telling of tongue' (Hopkins), and its sheer unmerited character, was cause of endless fascination and awe. Cradled in the hollow of her lover's hand, she thrilled to the experience of hope and courage and power. In times of suffering and disaster she came to know the tender and vulnerable quality of that love. When she failed to return love for love, her lover did not abandon her but offered forgiveness and a new beginning that extended even to establishing a new covenant on her behalf. Even in the pain of unrequited love, the bridegroom was ever active to bring about a profoundly new and exciting future for her. 'Behold, I am doing a new thing.' (Is 43:19)

It is not surprising then that God is described as 'merciful and gracious, long-suffering and rich in *hesed* (loving-kindness or steadfast love), and faithfulness'. Many commentators stress that *hesed* is the quality which marks off covenant religion and morality, for it highlights the steadfastness, fidelity and loyalty of God in covenant relationship. This is true, but we must remember that this is not something that comes into existence only when the covenant is established, it is rather what makes the covenant, and Israel's response to it, possible. (Hos 2:19) Israel is expected to respond in *hesed*, to God's free and gracious *hesed* (Hos 10:12, Jer 31:3) – which is no more than what lovers recognise spontaneously. ('Because you have loved me you have made me lovable.' *St Augustine.*) But even when she fails, God, out of faithfulness to God's *hesed*, remains freely bound to her and this becomes the basis for her hope and confidence in a new beginning. It is the *hesed* of this God, who is for life and against death in all its forms and disguises, that quite simply makes life possible. Accordingly, it becomes the motive for worship and in liturgical assembly the refrain, 'His steadfast *hesed* endures for ever' is ceaselessly proclaimed. This word is translated into English, albeit inadequately, as grace or graciousness.

Emet

Hesed is frequently twinned with another word, *emet*, which communicates a sense of dependability, sureness, confidence, faithfulness and security. When human beings act with *emet* their friendship and support is 'firm and immovable as a rock'. They are truthful in all their dealings. These qualities are understood to be verified absolutely in God's relationship to Israel – God, as the unshakeable foundation of all that is, is utterly faithful and absolutely truthful and reliable. This brings to mind the close affinity between *hesed* and *rahamim*.

Rahamim

Rehem means a mother's womb (or the location of the deepest feelings in a man). *Rahamim* speaks of the spontaneous, visceral attachment of mother or father to the child of womb or loins, or the special affection felt between those who have emerged from the same womb 'and breasts they have sucked the same' (Hopkins). By way of extension, it means the tender, vulnerable response to another, the heartfelt empathy for another's need

that wells up from the core of one's being. In English we translate it as 'mercy' or more adequately as 'compassion'. Yahweh,
the Creator God, is said to turn constantly to Israel as the created
one in *rahamim*. Even in the face of her rejection, Yahweh continues to love her in fidelity to God's own *rahamim*. 'Can a woman
forget her sucking child that she should have no compassion on
the child of her womb? Even these may forget yet I will not forget you.' (Is 49:15) Paired with *hesed*, it points to the maternal
vulnerability of God's love.

Sedaqa

Closely linked to *hesed* too is *sedaqa*. Whether it is translated as
justice or justification or repentance, we must remember that it
has had a very difficult and complex history in both the Jewish
and Christian traditions. It refers to standards maintained,
promises and obligations fulfilled, benefits received in relationships, and so its connection with other words seen so far is obvious. It connotes carrying out a project or providing a service
with dedication and with loyalty, thereby not only acting justly
but being seen to be *saddiq*, just. *Sedaqa* is such a precious but
vulnerable quality that elaborate measures must be taken to restore it if it is impinged in any way. (Ex 23:7f, Deut 25:1-3) At
times even these measures do not restore righteousness and the
religious person is thrown back on the *sedaqa* of God. In several
psalms, Yahweh is addressed as 'the God of my righteousness'
and possessing *sedaqa* 'in the eyes of' such a God is very important. God's *sedaqa* is not concerned primarily with passing judgement or repaying in strict measure, but ensuring that things are
as they should be, that they are 'right'. It is stressed that even
when righteousness disappears from the land, God is faithful to
the covenant and fulfils its promise because of fidelity to God's
own *sedaqa*. (Jer 4:1f, Zeph 2:3) Here *sedaqa* virtually coincides
with 'salvation' and is indeed frequently translated into Greek
as salvation or redemption. In some passages of the bible, the
emphasis is on the *sedaqa* created by those who have lived out
the covenant in fidelity and are innocent of wrongdoing.

This link between upright action and well-being or salvation in
life was of the utmost significance for Israelites and yet was the
subject of the most profound questioning (Job, Qoheleth,
Sirach). Towards the end of First Testament times, we find the

beginnings of a contrast between the 'official' position, where God justifies the righteous ones, not the sinners, and the newly emergent conviction that God's *sedaqa* is manifested in justification by grace, not by virtue of works. This debate will move centre stage in St Paul's writings.

Salvation

It has been mentioned above that at a certain stage 'salvation' and *sedaqa* could be used interchangeably, but this is true as well of the other key concepts analysed so far. The basic image underpinning the Hebrew (and common sense) notion which is translated as 'salvation' is that of space. 'To save' means to provide a safe place, to be roomy, to be broad, and it is opposed to all that 'cribs, cabins or confines' or that weakens or oppresses or enslaves. The reality to which the word 'salvation' refers is always conditioned by the experience of the absence of salvation, so this reality can never be static; it is ever-expanding, ever-deepening. It stretches from liberation from the minor discomforts of life, through forgiveness of sin to resurrection of the dead. Obviously to the Hebrew imagination none of these achievements is possible without the gracious, creative, steadfast, faithful love of Yahweh. In other words, all of what has been uncovered so far is inextricably linked and should not be separated. Those who translated the bible into Greek clearly recognised this unity and at times rendered one concept in terms of another.

This translation was no easy task. It is not simply a matter of translating a word or a phrase accurately into another language, but of communicating the very heart of a symbol-system, of articulating an entire spirituality founded on and suffused by God's graciousness.

Charis

At first sight the Greek *charis* seems the obvious candidate to translate *hanan* or *hesed* but in fact the term most frequently used for both is *eleos* (mercy). *Charis* is derived from a root which means to gleam or to sparkle and so denotes whatever delights, attracts, charms, gives pleasure and brings joy. Beauty, elegance, gracefulness and so on may generate that favourable impression, and the benevolence and favour which are likely to follow are also called *charis*. *Charis* is understood always to call forth a response of *charis*. In the classical Greek tradition, *charis* was not a particularly important word, had not been pressed in to service as a religious term, and never included the forgiveness of sins. Presumably it was these limitations, combined with its stress on the qualities of the one who possesses *charis* rather than its source, that made it unsuitable as an equivalent for *hesed*. The affinities between *charis* and *hen*, however, were obvious to the septuagint translators and they rendered it accordingly. Yet these decisions were not irreformable and in the later Wisdom literature *charis* begins to be used to refer to God's present and future reward. In that milieu, the gift of God's law to Israel was spoken of as God's greatest *charis* and when gentiles become children of the law through conversion, they were described as 'finding grace (*charis*) with God'. Here too *charis* is seen as an exemplification of God's loving mercy (*eleos*) which justifies sinners and is understood as salvation in the deepest sense.

We notice how *charis* is attracting all the cognate meanings discussed so far and is retrieving all the resonances of *hesed*. *Charis* can be used even to translate *hesed* and that is the meaning that is carried forward into New Testament times. Interestingly too, in that same milieu, we find the beginnings of the debate about justification (is it by grace or works?) which will loom large in Paul's writings concerning the contrast between the grace of the law and the grace of Christ. Finally, this period witnessed a new awareness of Israel's sinfulness as the greatest obstacle to salvation. As alienation from the gracious God of the covenant, it was foreclosing her real future. There was also a deepening demand for consistent *hesed*, integrity and justice from each individual, and with it the promise of forgiveness, reconciliation and an exciting new beginning.

Summary
It is refreshing to turn to what the First Testament has to say about Israel's experience of the graciousness of God, especially if one's mind has been exposed to the clutter of dry and arid divisions and distinctions that characterise the scholastic theology of grace. Here, by contrast, there are no distinctions between natural and supernatural – the delivery from Egypt and safe delivery in childbirth are both equally the gracious gifts of God.

Nor do we find any trace of the tiresome attempts to categorise different kinds of grace – it is living and vibrant, transforming and ordinary. 'Everything is grace.' (Philo) Neither are there any sharp distinctions between God the giver and the gift given – it passes over into the beloved while still remaining God's own. The beloved receives freely but is transformed in the process and is expected to reflect what has been received. The dialectic of divine initiative and human refusal and failure, which are the warp and woof of Israel's history, serves to highlight the poignant, unconditional quality of this love. The powerful vocabulary which we have examined was crafted by a people captivated by their experience of the creative, salvific, self-giving love of this God. They name that love as fabulous, faithful and utterly gracious. The creators of that rich vocabulary sought to express in a single word the most important dimension of cosmos and history, of life and liturgy, and the word chosen was 'grace'.

2. The New Testament

Jesus[2]

If we turn to the New Testament and check the references to 'grace', we will be disappointed. There is no word for grace in Mark; Matthew has the word *eleos* three times; Luke uses *eleos* seven times (though it is not used in a technical sense) and *charis* is found four times in the prologue to John's gospel. However, even if the words for grace occur infrequently, every iota of the gospel is about grace. Jesus of Nazareth is presented in the gospels as the exemplary recipient of God's *hanan, hesed, rahamim* and *sedaqa* and the inexhaustible source of them for others. We noted above how these realities were lavished in a special way on the poor, the weak, the undeserving, and in the gospels we are told that it was precisely these people that Jesus seeks out and gathers to himself. To them he proclaims the kingdom/reign of God, with unshakeable conviction and provocative originality. When we listen to the language he uses to hint at the reign of God active in life, we must realise that it articulates first of all Jesus' own experience of total yet gracious dependence on God. He is captivated by this God who has first loved him and whom he names in responding love as Abba. Seeing everything through the eyes of the Beloved, he declares this God to be pas-

sionately in love with all women and men. The dream of this
lover of humanity is for what is best for all, 'that they might have
life and have it to the full'. (Jn 10:10) The powerful images and
metaphors of his persuasive and provocative parables enable
the reign of that gracious God to take shape. Using images
which speak of lavish bounty, prodigal graciousness, superabundant compassion, he seeks to communicate the mystery of
that God to his hearers. Through imaginative interaction with
these stories, they are given a glimpse of the reign of a God who
is utterly gracious and infinitely merciful.

Jesus speaks of God as the tender, compassionate Abba whose
heart goes out to all his children, not because they deserve it, but
quite simply because they are his children. We notice too how
frequently *rahamim*, compassion, womb-love, is said to characterise the response of a central character in his stories, or Jesus'
own response, to others.

The praxis of the kingdom

Jesus is presented to us as a man of intense faith in the faithful
graciousness of God (*emet*) who trusts the Abba 'who sees what
is done in secret' even when there seems to be no human basis
for that hope. In turn, he graciously invites others to entrust
themselves, through him, to the protective love of this God, 'to
come' to him when they 'labour and are overburdened'. The
voice of the kingdom becomes credible when the one who proclaims God's *sedaqa* stands in scandalising solidarity with the
marginals of the holiness system, to the point of opposition to
the law. His humane praxis of the kingdom delivered the poor,
the oppressed and the suffering from their alienation and pain.
The kingdom becomes enfleshed in the miracles and exorcisms
of Jesus, as he lavishes God's prodigal love on the afflicted. He
had the ability to create the space around himself in which the
outcasts of society, the despised, the broken, the lost, experienced communion with each other and with God.

The dark side of Jesus' proclamation is the judgement that much
of what obtained within the holiness system was not in accord
with the calculus of *hesed* (was it an embodiment of *hen*?), was
not in harmony with God's dream, was opposed to *sedaqa*. Jesus
invites all those who are denied justice within the religious insti-

tutions of the day to throw themselves on God's *sedaqa*. To disciples he proposed a renewed vision that would be in harmony with that *sedaqa*, and a practical way of being together which would implement that vision.

His most powerful symbolic enactment of his lived conviction about God's graciousness took place at table under the invocation of God's blessing. That action proclaimed dramatically that there were no outsiders to God's reign. By eating and drinking together in such circumstances, Jesus enabled his companions to feel in their very guts (the place of *rahamim*) the difference that could be made by his new vision of God and humanity. They experienced it as a pure gracious gift. Others looked askance at what he did and saw it as the work of the anti-Christ. Opposition to him mounted and finally he was arrested and crucified.

Disciples who fled in self-serving fear from his cross, who betrayed him and left him to die alone, insisted after Easter that something radical had happened to them because something indescribable had happened to him. They maintain that their discipleship had been renewed because Jesus who had been crucified had not been held by death. God had graciously sustained him even in the deadliness of death and had 'raised him up' to new life at the heart of God. This did not mean that he was removed from contact with them but rather that the totality of his life, death and new life were graciously made present to them, again, only because of the absolute gratuitousness of God's loving initiative or *hesed*.

The disciples had abandoned Jesus in his hour of need, they had let him down because of self-interest and cowardice, they had been inconsistent at the time of crisis. No doubt their pathetic failure left them with feelings of culpability and guilt. And after his death there appeared to be no way in which they could obtain forgiveness or reconciliation. So the presence of the crucified-risen Jesus to them must have been an indescribably intense and poignant experience of forgiveness, reconciliation, at-one-ment. It was salvation and grace in the most profound sense. It is tempting to say that they were re-established in the fellowship which they had sundered but to which he, with a love that proved stronger than death, remained faithful. But that runs the risk of concentrating over much on healing the past as past. In the Easter stories, the communication from the crucified-risen

One does not accuse and never harps on the past, but the offer of forgiveness after their disloyalty happens through the utter graciousness of his new presence to them. They may indeed have thought of Jesus as finally dead; now they realised that they were the ones who had passed through the death of their 'discipleship' into a new 'following' of him, as the crucified-risen One. This new commitment to him as definitive source of forgiveness, salvation, healing and wholeness in the power of the Spirit, involved a total conversion that completely restructured their hearts and lives. They were never satisfied simply to state what this transformation meant; they felt compelled above all to struggle to incarnate it by passionately pursuing what Jesus of Nazareth had embodied in his ministry.

The disciples did not understand immediately the full implications of what had happened to the crucified Jesus, and through him to them, but they realised right from the start that it involved a disclosure of the very being of God's self. This utterly gratuitous act of God on behalf of the crucified Jesus, who had lived in utter dependence on God, is the supreme and final grace, it is the definitive act of salvation. If the God of Jesus did not allow him to be held by death, then that God has been revealed as the one true God who alone raises the dead. This is the faithful God of fabulous surprises whose righteousness and mercy as Lord and giver of new life have been vindicated. This God's passionate concern for the future of humanity has been revealed, for in the crucified Jesus humanity has broken through to a future that fulfils all human hopes and dreams. 'There is salvation in no one else, for there is no other name under heaven given among women and men by which we must be saved.' (Acts 4:12) So the good news of the risen–crucified Jesus and the God who raised him to new life can and must be proclaimed, in the power of God's spirit, as salvation and judgement to the whole human race and not only to Jews. In this mission the evangelisers will wrestle with images, symbols, metaphors and concepts from both the Jewish and gentile worlds in order to bring that mystery to expression. Saul of Tarsus, persecutor of the infant church, who became Paul, the apostle to the gentiles and theologian of that same church, played a crucial role in that process. It is to his writings that we must now turn.

Grace and salvation in the writings of St Paul
Even a cursory review of Paul's writings would convince us that *charis*/grace is a characteristically Pauline word. By contrast with its infrequent occurrence in the gospels, it is found about one hundred times in Paul's letters. If we add to this the many cognate words such as 'salvation', 'righteousness', 'mercy', 'glory', 'redemption', etc. which he uses, we realise that we are faced with a complex and formidable vocabulary. It would not be helpful simply to exegete these references nor to endeavour to organise this material according to themes, nor even to attempt to pursue a putative theme called 'grace' in his letters. *Charis*/grace is not a discrete theme in Paul's writings and it does not have a single, clearly-defined consistent meaning. It is a lode-word of extraordinary depth and density and range of meaning, but a word which will remain largely unintelligible and unappreciated unless it is linked constantly to its origins in the Jewish Testament. A few examples should serve to hint at that trajectory of meaning.

It was usual in the conventions of letter-writing in Greek to begin with the salutation, *Chaire*, Hail (health and well-being), but through a clever word-play Paul deepens this to '*Charis* to you and peace from God our Father and the Lord Jesus Christ' – the greeting that we find in many of his letters. Used as a form of leavetaking at the end of his letters it burgeons towards benediction and this reaches its most elaborate expression in 'The grace of the Lord Jesus Christ and the love of God and the fellowship of the Holy Spirit be with you all.' (2 Cor 13:14)

In other places he uses it to describe the collection he is taking up on behalf of the poor in Jerusalem (1 Cor 16:3; 2 Cor 8:1-7,19) asking the Corinthians to reflect by their generosity the *charis* of Jesus Christ who had so enriched them. On occasion a weak translation of *charis* into English as 'thanks' (e.g. Rom 7:25, 2 Cor 8:16) conceals its real meaning. For in such texts Paul is not only giving thanks for the gift he has received but is also gratefully acknowledging the gracious source of what he has received. Here the sense is of 'grace received and referred back' (awkward as it may sound in English) rather than an innane 'thanks' and so is very close to *eucharistia*, eucharist, ritual thanksgiving. (1 Cor 1:4, 11:17f, 2 Cor 4:15)

Sometimes he uses *charis* as a code-word for all that he has received so gratuitously and now offers so generously to others, 'the grace of Christ' that is the driving force of his calling and mission. But most distinctively he uses it as a word of symbolic density to summarise the overall perspective of his life, his teaching, his ministry. Through it he seeks to communicate what he has experienced as the most awesome and rapturous quality of God's relationship to humanity – its sheer, untrammelled generosity and gratuity.

Cornelius Ernst summarised Paul's use of *charis* as follows: 'We might say that he used it poetically, meaning that under the pressure of powerful enthusiastic feeling, the word excited associations and even perhaps created them when Paul set about preaching the gospel of God's transcendent generosity to man in Jesus Christ ... To understand Paul's use of 'grace' we have to try to reconstitute an experience, not to analyse an idea'.[3] What was that experience?

Experience at Damascus

A portentous, critical incident took place in the life of Saul of Tarsus, near Damascus. That experience deconstructed his life up to that point, reconstructed it completely and opened up an entirely new life that previously had seemed unthinkable. We saw above how important it was to acknowledge the radical conversion undergone by the foundational members of the 'Way' of Jesus if we are to understand their ministry and teaching. Their discipleship is indeed re-created but, in retrospect at least, we may discern a substantial continuity. Saul's conversion by comparison is unique. Unlike them, he appears not to have had any contact with the historical Jesus. If he heard of him he would have judged him, presumably, to be a false prophet opposing Israel's God, subverting her faith and relativising the law of Moses. No doubt he would have believed that the falsity of Jesus' preaching and action had been proven by his death as a religious reprobate on the cross. Anyway, we know that in the name of God (as Saul then understood God), he began with great zeal to persecute those who were perfidiously claiming that Jesus, who died a death reserved for those accursed by God (Deut 21:23), was alive in new way. During one such foray against the followers of 'The Way', something happened to Saul that changed everything, utterly. There is no discernible continuity in his life between the 'before and after' of this experience. (Any possible continuity could only be found in God and in the witnesses he persecuted and then joined.) The emphasis is rather on an unbridgeable discontinuity. This archetypal experience transformed totally all that made Saul Saul, and it left an indelible stamp on everything he said and did from then on. We could hardly overestimate the significance of this experience for Paul and, in a sense, all of his teaching and writing are a series of footnotes to this event.

Luke narrates that experience of Saul three times in Acts (9, 22, 26) and, despite discrepancies concerning attendant details the core dialogue is substantially the same. 'Saul, Saul, Why do you persecute me?' – 'Who are you, Sir?' – 'I am Jesus whom you are persecuting.' The Lord appears or is revealed to him as the crucified-risen-persecuted One. As in the case of the others who had similar experiences, the overwhelming gratuitousness of this revelation must be stressed first of all. But given its prehistory, the indescribable poignancy of that encounter cries out to be acknowledged. We might wish to characterise it further as being an experience which was simultaneously both gracious salvation and fearful judgement and perhaps it was. But we must remember that, for Paul himself, it was the qualities of undeserved graciousness and unmerited forgiveness which unquestionably dominate in his recall of that genetic moment.

It was this revelation of the crucified-risen-persecuted Jesus as forgiveness that turned Saul around from service of a God whom he thought needed persecutors, to service of the persecuted God and that God's persecuted Son. Others said of him 'He who once persecuted us is now preaching the faith he once tried to destroy.' (Gal 1:23) He became a 'servant of Christ' (Gal 1:10) as a result of that 'revelation of Jesus Christ' (Gal 1:12), the crucified 'Lord of Glory' (1 Cor 2:8). He spoke of it as being 'seized or made his own' by Christ Jesus (Phil 3:12) and again of God being 'pleased to reveal his Son to me.' (Gal 1:16) It was such an awesome experience that he compares it to God's first creative act: 'For it is the God who said "Let light shine out of darkness" who has shone in our hearts to give the light of the knowledge of the glory of God in the face of Christ'. (2 Cor 4:6) He sees it as a foundational event that gave him the same status as that which the twelve enjoyed – 'Am I not an apostle? Have I not seen Jesus,

Our Lord?' (1 Cor 9:1) – even if he were 'untimely born'. (1 Cor 15:8) And like the twelve (and the others) he too was driven by a compulsion to preach the good news, 'for necessity is laid upon me'. (1 Cor 9:16)

Preaching the good news

When preaching the 'good news of the glory of Christ' (2 Cor 44), Paul could speak with powerful authority about the radical contrast between his former existence and his new life 'in Christ'. It was his wish that others would go through a process of conversion similar to what he had undergone. He was concerned that his hearers, like himself, would come to know the implications of the death and resurrection of Jesus Christ and respond to them in faith, by committing their lives totally to him. It is not surprising then that the strategy he uses is to contrast the transforming graciousness of the new life made available through Christ with the darkness and despair of life without him. (Rom 6:22, 76, 1 Cor 6:9-11, Gal 4:8-9) He needs to emphasise humankind's desperate need for salvation in order to highlight the overwhelming and surpassing salvation that has come through Jesus Christ – 'where sin increased grace abounded all the more'. (Rom 5:20) To speak about the need for salvation is to speak about the mysteries of suffering and death, about finitude, helplessness, failure, guilt and sin. But because evil in this broad sense is so elusive, formless, indiscrete, 'respectable', all-pervasive yet hidden and inevitable, any attempt to expose as evil what masquerades as good needs the mediation of symbol, story and metaphor. ('Because there is evil, there are symbols.' P. Ricoeur). Paul certainly uses powerful symbols in dramatic form.

Life without Christ

In the 'Drama of Salvation', Act 1: 'Life without Christ', he pictures Everyperson as frail and vulnerable, incapable of living as they should – this is what he calls 'living according to the flesh' (Rom 8:12), and in his presentation they are surrounded, indwelt and dominated by destructive and hostile forces and powers. He names these powerful, diabolic (as opposed to symbolic) forces as Sin, Death and the Law. These three are virtually personified in his writings. (Rather like the way we speak of 'Capitalism' and 'Communism'.) He distinguishes between Sin and 'transgression' or 'trespasses', (which we might call sins) and sees the latter as the concrete expressions of the deeper reality, Sin. This underlying reality is hostile to God, refuses to recognise the first commandment and instead urges worship of the self, leaving Everyperson unfree and unfulfilled. It dominates everyone and any struggle to overcome it only entraps them more deeply in its moils. It suffuses and distorts everything and while expressing itself in obviously sinful actions, it can vitiate even the pursuit of ultimate wisdom or the quest for righteousness.

Paul draws on the powerful symbolism of the Adamic story to 'explain' how, through Adam, the power of Sin was unleashed into the world. It enables him also to speak about the unity of the human race and its solidarity in evil, failure and sin. (Rom 5:12) From this he can build up a lamentable picture of both Jewish and gentile history where evil abounds and sin is heaped contagiously on sin. (Rom 1:18ff)

He again relies on the Adamic story to link Sin and Death very closely. Death is a tyrannical force, oppressing and enslaving Everyperson. Paul is not thinking primarily about biological death in itself, but rather about the terror generated in Everyperson in the face of death because their lives are sin-dominated. This anxiety about and preoccupation with Death is so all-pervasive that it exists as an independent force which gains painful expression through biological death. Because of sin, Everyperson is alienated from God, self and others and they know that in biological death that alienation may become final, Death may become total death.

The final *persona* in this drama is the Law. Here Paul's script is more nuanced. The Law is good in itself, a grace from God, designed to lead those privileged to know it 'to choose life' with God. Yet it too enslaved people because it could only point the way externally towards life, it was incapable of providing the force or power needed to liberate those 'old under sin'. (Rom 7:14) This impotence of the Law only added to the Israelites' guilt and sense of failure and condemnation. (Knowing what to do but being unable to do it (Rom 7:25) and, like the gentiles, they too 'sinned and fell short of the glory of God'. (Rom 3:23))

Because the Law was taken in train by Sin, and Everyperson as 'carnal (*sarkinos*) and sold under sin' (Rom 7:14) was unable to resist it, Paul can even say 'The Law came in to increase transgressions'. (Rom 5:20) Here Paul is drawing on his own deepest experiences.

Looking back on his youth, Paul recalls that he was 'circumcised on the eighth day of the tribe of Benjamin, a Hebrew born of the Hebrews; as to the law a Pharisee, as to zeal a persecutor of the church, as to righteousness under the law, blameless.' (Phil 3:5-6) Like all human beings, he lived under the shadow of death and like them he would have known the weakness and frailty of the human condition (*sarx*, 'flesh'). No doubt even one so priggishly self-righteous as Saul knew the meaning of transgression but would have believed that strict observance of the law's demands would ensure salvation.

At Damascus, while carrying out a mission that was commendable in terms of the law, he encountered the one whom he judged to be the sinful anti-Christ and whose memory he sought to obliterate, Jesus the crucified-risen-persecuted One. This experience turned Paul's life and world upside down and inside out. What he had taken as the pursuit of uprightness was now revealed as opposed to God's very Self and manifested the extent to which he was possessed by Sin and threatened by Death. No doubt he would have applauded those who handed over Jesus of Nazareth to be crucified, but it was now revealed that they had 'crucified the Lord of glory' (1 Cor 1:8) and that he himself had continued that process by persecuting followers of his 'Way'. Yet it was this same Saul who was being graced by this revelation and thereby knew himself to be loved unconditionally, to be forgiven and reconciled at the deepest level. The vulnerable nature of that love and lover is communicated through the question that is asked, 'Why do you persecute me?' And even when it takes the shape of crucified love, it continues to love those who crucify, oppress and persecute. As a graced sinner, Saul came to know a righteousness or uprightness that certainly did not depend on works done in accordance with the law. That revelation was for Saul the beginning of the 'New Creation' and he became a new creature. Nothing in his life had prepared him for the radical newness of that experience, nothing that he had ever done deserved such an initiative. It was an utter, incomprehensible, inexpressible gift which could come only from the sheer graciousness of God's unconditional love.

The response to this transforming experience did not come from Saul's resources either; it too is equally 'a gift' of God. The One who graciously granted the revelation, graciously enables the recipient to respond. This is what Paul calls faith. He certainly does not mean being internally enthusiastic about a new idea or merely giving assent to propositions, but rather a God-sustained response of the whole person – intellect, will, emotions – to this revelation of God.

In his presentation of the human situation, Paul succeeded brilliantly in bringing to light what exists at the deepest level, and unmasking as evil what rejoices in honourable names. And he has shown convincingly that while Everyperson needs to be rescued and liberated, and while the enemies, Sin and Death, must be overcome, such salvation could not come from within the human community as such. But it is not enough for someone to successfully symbolise the evil that is truly there in people's lives. This will leave the hearers with only a tragic and hopeless reading of the situation which then becomes even more intolerable because all cushioning illusions have been destroyed. What is needed instead to counterpose a more powerful positive reading of that situation, which will show how the evil inherent in it can be overcome. This is precisely what Paul does and it is good news indeed.

Life in Christ

His gospel is that 'God's love has been poured into our hearts through the Holy Spirit that has been given to us'. (Rom 5:5) This is 'The Drama of Salvation', Act II: 'Salvation in Christ'. Paul sees that what has taken place through Christ Jesus addresses and overcomes in a surpassing way the situation that prevailed in Act I. 'Now, then, there is no condemnation for those who are in Christ Jesus, for the law of the Spirit of life has freed me from the law of sin and death. For God has done what the law, weakened by flesh, could not do: He sent his own Son in the likeness of sinful flesh in order that the just requirement of the law might be achieved in us who walk not according to the flesh but according to the Spirit'. (Rom 8:1-4)

Paul believed that Jesus Christ had struggled with all the destructive forces depicted in Act I of his drama. He saw him as fully involved in the human situation, as 'descended from David according to the flesh' (Rom 1:3), 'born of a woman, born under the law'. (Gal 4:4) It was obvious too that he was subject to death. Throughout his ministry he had come into conflict with those upholding the strict letter of the law and was put to death in its name. The tyrannical forces of Sin and Death, ever active in the life of Everyperson, carried their onslaught against Jesus even to death on a cross. That death appeared to be total subjugation to those powers but Paul was now absolutely convinced that Jesus Christ overcame those destructive forces (2 Cor 13:4) through consistent, loving fiselity to the Father. His response, Paul says, was 'always yes, for all the promises of God find their yes in him'. (2 Cor 1:19-20) So even Jesus' death was never in danger of becoming Death, it was rather his final passing over into the mystery of God.

Paul had little interest in the details of Jesus' life and ministry, but he could proclaim all this with certainty, for if it were not so, he could not have encountered him as 'Lord of glory' (1 Cor 2:8), 'established in power' (Rom 1:3-4). And because the crucified Jesus who was bone of our bone, flesh of our flesh, is now at the heart of the mystery of God, he sees him as 'the guarantee' (2 Cor 1:22), the 'first fruits' (1 Cor 15:20, Rom 8:23) of the ingathering of all humanity, 'the first born of many brothers and sisters'. (Rom 8:29)

In Act I, he had drawn on the Adamic story to stress the unity of the race in sin, alienation and distress. Now, by contrast, he speaks of the unity of reconciled humanity in Christ. 'Just as through one man's disobedience the many were made sinners, through one man's obedience the many would be made righteous'. (Rom 5:18) What happened when 'Jesus Our Lord was put to death for our trespasses and raised for our justification' (Rom 4:25) has made a difference to Everyperson. The history of the world is reversed, for Jesus Christ is the new Adam, the head of the new redeemed humanity, who 'has become a life-giving Spirit'. (1 Cor 15:45)

As Paul sees it, there are two realms or regimes, one headed by Adam, where sin, death and the law hold sway, the other infinitely superior, under the headship of Christ, where 'our wisdom, our righteousness, our sanctification and our redemption' (1 Cor 1:30) are found. The realm of law and the realm of grace are contrasted. The spirit of Christ breathes into humanity the breath of 'newness of life' (Rom 6:4) and makes of anyone in Christ 'a new creation' (2 Cor 5:17). In his own case, Paul experienced this to such a degree that he can say, 'It is no longer I who live but Christ lives in me; and the life I now live in the flesh I live by faith in the Son of God who loved me and gave himself for me'. (Gal 2:20) But he believes that this symbiosis exists between Christ and all those joined to him through faith and baptism, and he never tires of seeking to give expression to it throughout his letters. The 'Body of Christ' is the most startling figure that he uses to communicate the realism of his convictions. In some texts it may imply little more than moral union between members of the community but in some instances it goes beyond that to somehow include the organic, indeed the corporal levels as well. He reminds the Corinthians that: 'By one Spirit we are all baptised into one body – Jews or Greeks, slaves or free – and all were made to drink of one Spirit.' (12:13) This union is so close that he can describe it as being in 'one flesh' (6:16-17) and, in speaking to them about the eucharist, Paul affirms the shared-union that it creates among those who celebrate it and 'partake of the one bread' ... 'we who are many are One body.' (10:17) Negatively, he insists that if they do not discern or evaluate the authenticity of the relationships within the Body, then they 'divide Christ' by their egotistical behaviour when they assemble for the Lord's Supper and they are guilty of continuing the crucifixion of Jesus Christ. (11:17)

The good news
The core of the good news or gospel (a word he uses forty-eight times) preached by Paul is the word or story of the cross, which is 'folly to those who are perishing but to us who are being saved it is the power of God'. (1 Cor 1:18) He expands on this by saying, 'It pleased God through the folly of what we preach to save those who believe. For Jews demands signs, the Greeks wisdom but we preach Christ crucified. A stumbling block to Jews and a folly to gentiles but to those of us who are called, both Jews and Greeks, it is Christ the power of God and the wisdom of God'. (1 Cor 1:21-25) This revelation of God's salvific plan of ingathering

both Jews and gentiles through Christ Jesus, he calls 'God's mystery', hidden in God from eternity but now made visible. Paul sees 'the story of the cross' establishing a new righteousness or justification of human beings which does not calculate or repay in strict measure but acquits out of love. Unlike the old regime under the law, there 'is therefore now no condemnation for those in Christ Jesus' (Rom 8:1), they are no longer 'under the law but under grace'. (Rom 6:15) He sees the crucified-risen Jesus receiving all power from the Father and releasing it into the world so that believers may now do freely what was impossible under the dispensation of the law. (Rom 8:3) New righteousness, new faith, new love, new hope, new life, new freedom to do good, new holiness, new adoptive sonship and daughtership, are possible now because 'God's love has been poured into our hearts through the Holy Spirit who has been given to us'. (Rom 5:5)

Justification
This new way Paul describes climactically as 'being justified by grace as a gift, through the redemption which is in Christ Jesus ... to be received by faith'. (Rom 3:24-25, See Gal 2:16, 3:24) He is arguing emphatically from his own experience that it is God alone, in accordance with God's own *sedaqa*, that justifies the sinner, 'and all are sinners' (Rom 3:23), and enables them to stand before the divine judgement seat as 'upright and justified'. Against the Judaisers who maintained that converts would have to observe the law in order to achieve righteousness and justification, Paul points out that the cross shows how people who were faultless and ethically correct according to the works of the law, were nevertheless responsible for the death of Jesus. So, using their language but giving it an entirely new content, he argues that this 'new righteousness' through Christ crucified cannot be achieved through works of the law (Rom 3:28), but it is free and unmerited and must be accepted as a gift, in faith. To attempt to go back to the old dispensation is to 'nullify the grace of God; for if justification were through the law, then Christ died to no purpose'. (Gal 2:21) The point of entry into the new dispensation, he insists, is through faith – responding to the gospel, recognising the total mystery of Christ and committing the whole self in faith to that mystery. And that faith is not a verbal

or emotional thing; it means coming under the Spirit's law of love, so it must always be 'faith working itself out through love'. (Gal 5:6)

Paul's own faith was ritualised and ratified publicly when he was baptised into the community of faith in Christ Jesus. He teaches that through baptism the converts are being initiated into the death, burial and resurrection of Jesus Christ: 'We were buried therefore with him by baptism into death, so that as Christ was raised from the dead by the glory of the Father, we too might walk in newness of life. For if we have been united with him in a death like his, we shall certainly be united with him in a resurrection like his.' (Rom 6:4-5) In this way the pattern of Christian life, of dying and rising with Christ, is established. And that pattern must be lived out in a community which mediates the risen Christ. Christians find the centre of their existence in Christ, which means co-existence with all those who also draw life from the one source, Christ. This identity of Christ and the Christians was the first truth Saul learned – 'Why do you persecute me?'

Cosmic implications

So far, we have concentrated on Paul's presentation of the historical, personal and social implications of God's mysterious plan of salvation in Christ. He also acknowledges its cosmic implications in passages which speak about 'all things being subjected to him' (1 Cor 15:27, Phil 3:21) and sees all of creation being involved in the process of liberation (Rom 8:19-21). In the Deutero-Pauline letters to the Colossians and Ephesians, this dimension is explored further and Christ is presented as the source, the sustainer, the meaning and the goal of all creation (See Col 1:15-18, Eph 1:19-23). In a powerful passage that brings together many Pauline themes, the Ephesians are told that 'God who is rich in mercy, out of the great love with which he loved us even when we were dead through our trespasses, made us alive together with Christ (by grace you have been saved), and raised us up with him and made us sit with him in the heavenly places in Christ Jesus, that in the coming ages he might show the immeasurable riches of his grace in kindness towards us in Christ Jesus. For by grace you have been saved through faith; and this is not your own doing, it is the gift of God – not because

of works lest anyone should boast.' (2:4-9) In the same chapter
they are reminded that Christ Jesus 'is our peace, who has made
us both (Jews and gentiles) one and has broken down the dividing wall of hostility, by abolishing in his flesh the law of commandments and ordinances that he might create in himself one
new person in place of two, so making peace ...' (14-15)

Summary
In the Pauline writings there is no systematic treatment of a topic
called 'grace'. Rather it seems that he uses the word to hint at
what is most distinctive about the mode of God's relationship to
the world and in particular to the human race. When he reviews
the entire sweep of the gift of God's Self to cosmos and history,
he is so overawed by it that he can only repeat the word *charis*, as
a noun, a verb, an adjective, an adverb, even to the point of taut-
ology – we have been graced gratuitously by God's gracious
favour. 'It is not as though we were to itemise God's gifts and
call one of them 'grace'; it is rather that 'grace' qualifies the
whole of God's self-communication as a gift beyond all telling'.[4]

Grace and salvation in the Johannine writings
The word *charis*/grace occurs four times in the prologue to
John's gospel. It is not found elsewhere in the body of the gospel
or the first and third letters. It's meaning, where it does occur in
the second letter (3) and in the Apocalypse (1:4) is that of a con-
ventional greeting.

When the prologue attempts to summarise the revelation that
has taken place in the 'Word-made-flesh', he is described as
being 'full of grace and truth' (1:14,17) and as the One from
whose 'fullness have we all received grace upon grace' (1:16).
These summary statements should alert us to the all-pervasive
reality of *charis*/grace in the gospel, even where the word is not
found. The same is true of the other Johannine writings.

'God so loved the world that he gave his only Son, that whoever
believes in him should not perish but have eternal life'. (3:16)
That verse is often described as 'the gospel in miniature', and it
certainly highlights the main emphases and concerns of John's
good news. It begins by recalling the deliberate loving initiative
of God, and continues, 'For God sent his Son into the world not

to condemn the world but that the world might be saved through him' (3:16-17), or again 'We love because he first loved us' (1 Jn 4:19). This God, through Jesus, the one and only Son, has offered definitive salvation to women and men. That salvation is not other than Jesus of Nazareth, he himself *is* salvation, 'the Saviour of the World'. (Jn 4:42,1 Jn 4:14) This is so because the Father who has loved him 'before the foundation of the world' (17:24) has given him everything (3:35, 13:3), even his 'name' (17:11-12) and his glory (17:22-24). 'No one has ever seen God; the only Son who is in the bosom of the Father, he made him known.' (1:18) Jesus, the one who has been 'sent', does nothing of his 'own authority' (5:30) but always and only the 'will' and the 'works' of the Father (4:34). So to see Jesus is to see the Father, for he and the Father are one. (10:30, 17:11,22) 'I have come that you may have life and have it abundantly'. (10:10) This symbol of 'life' is central in the gospel and, for John, grace or salvation means participating in the life of the Word-made-flesh. This intimate union with God is spoken of powerfully and dramatically as being 'begotten/born of God/Spirit' (1:12-13, 3:4-8) and is possible only because the Son of God has been born in 'the flesh' of our humanity. So the community of believers itself is generated and enlivened by communion with the Father and the Son, in the Spirit. This communion is made manifest among them when 'they love one another' as Jesus loved them. (13:34,35 15:12)

'God is love' (1 Jn 4:8, 16) and Jesus himself is the incarnation of that love and the perfect response to it. It is this love that comes from the Father (17:23-26) that Jesus offers gratuitously to all who believe in him and it is his prayer that they may be suffused by it. John uses 'love' to characterise all God's relationships with human beings, as Paul had used 'grace'. Love is also, for him, the quintessence of the believer's life. It is at the heart of what grace and salvation and discipleship mean. 'We know we have passed out of death into life because we love the brothers and sisters. The one who does not love remains in death.' (1 Jn 3:14)

The overwhelming graciousness of God towards us in the Word-made-flesh is seen as all the more astonishing when we remember the background against which it unfolds in the Johannine writings. In a way that is reminiscent of Paul, we discover that the story of what God has done through Jesus is enhanced through the use of contrasting polarities. We find not only contrast but open conflict between the heavenly and earthly worlds, life and death, love and hatred, above and below, freedom and slavery, light and darkness, spirit and flesh, truth and lies. Jesus is seen as conquering all these negativities from within. The kingdom of death, darkness, slavery and lies is overcome and Jesus' kingdom of life, love, freedom and truth is established. So contrary to appearances or to the 'view from below', 'the world' is overcome (16:33), his crucifixion is really his 'hour' when he is glorified by the Father, his being lifted up on the cross is his exaltation, his death is the beginning of life eternal. In this way he has opened up new life for believers who are enabled by him to pass out of the realm of death into the realm of new life. John insists that followers of the Word-made-flesh really share eternal life already (even if its fullness will be achieved only at the end-time). (3:15-16, 6:47,54)

They enter into this life through knowledge and faith: 'This is eternal life to know you, the only true God, and Jesus Christ whom you have sent'. (17:3) 'Knowing' here does not signify mere information or some kind of theoretical or practical understanding; it evinces a deep and intimate knowledge involving communion of life and is based on faith. Faith in turn is a God-given response to revelation that involves a radical commitment of the self to the One who is revealed.

The faith and knowledge of believers after Easter are themselves the gifts of the Spirit who 'will teach you all things and bring to your remembrance all that I have said to you'. (Jn 14:26)

The Spirit, as ever-abiding sanctifier, comes from the Father and the glorified Jesus (16:7) and is the principle of life in the community. The Spirit enables the disciples for whom John is writing to be just as surely in contact with the source of love and life that came through Jesus of Nazareth as his historical disciples were. The Spirit is powerfully active in the proclamation of the word in the community and presides over its celebrations of baptism and eucharist, symbolised by the blood and water that flowed from the side of the crucified-and-exalted Son of Man on the cross. Through baptism, new members are born again/from above, in 'water and the Spirit' (3:5) and, at the eucharist, they share in 'the flesh and blood' of the exalted Word-made-flesh, knowing that they 'who eat this bread will live forever'. (6:58) This is the bread of life.

It is not surprising then that the author of the prologue, in seeking to summarise in advance all that will be revealed in the gospel, says 'Grace and truth' (*hesed* and *emet*) happened or took dramatic shape in Jesus Christ (17) and that from his fullness has come 'grace upon grace' (16).

Finally, before leaving the documents of the New Testament, it is necessary to note one other text, 2 Peter 1:3-4, 'His divine power has granted to us all things that pertain to life and godliness, through the knowledge of him who called us to his own glory and excellence, by which he has granted to us his precious and great promises, that through these you may escape from the corruption that is in the world because of passion, and become partakers of the divine nature.' It is an important text, not because it offers an insight into filiation not otherwise available, but because of the use made of it by theologians in both East and West. In particular the phrase 'become partakers of/participants in the divine nature' was used widely in the East to support their theory of divinisation, and in the West it served almost as a definition of grace for scholastic theologians.

Notes

1. Besides the biblical dictionaries of the Old and New Testaments, and *The Jerome Biblical Commentary*, the following may be found useful: Reumann, J., *Righteousness in the New Testament*, Fortress Press 1982; Schillebeeckx, E., *Christ: The experience of Jesus as Lord*, Seabury, 1987; Soards, M., *The Apostle Paul: An Introduction to his writing and teaching*, Paulist Press, 1987.

2. A more extended treatment of the message and ministry of Jesus will be found in chapter 9.

3. *The Theology of Grace*, Mercier Press, 1974, 19.

4. ibid, 29.

CHAPTER SIX

Models of grace

'Footfalls echo in the memory
Down the passage which we did not take
Towards the door we never opened.'
(T. S. Eliot)

In the previous chapter we tried to uncover some of the richness of the scriptural material which attempts to communicate the reality of God's gracious desire to create and save. Through that perusal of the scriptures we were put in touch with the authors' own wonder and awe and fascination before the utter mystery of God's saving power. It is this awe and wonder which would find expression in their liturgical celebrations. We could hardly have avoided noticing the imaginative, creative and diverse ways in which they used images, symbols, metaphors, models and concepts to articulate their conviction about the prodigal graciousness of God. That rich pluralism of approaches was absolutely essential if the mysterious complexity of divine-human relations were to be acknowledged. Yet, because they were wrestling with the infinite intelligibility of that mystery, it would always defy all attempts at definition or description – 'Words after speech, reach into silence.' (Eliot) And beyond the inevitable inadequacy and inappropriateness of all human attempts to speak of God, was the realisation that the reality about which they spoke must be proclaimed and incarnated rather than merely stated. It was their conviction that only the fullness of transformed lives, lived out of that mystery and towards final union with it, could be adequate media for its expression. It would be in praxis and praise that the gracious mystery would be most appropriately acknowledged.

While we note these necessary limitations, we must cherish the fruits of their struggle to 'hint and guess' at the mystery of God's grace and salvation and be profoundly grateful for their legacy.

It would be impossible to overestimate the importance for us of the powerful images, metaphors and models which they have crafted, or to appreciate fully the influence of such images on our belief and behaviour, our praxis and praise.

Images
In a world and a culture bombarded constantly by images, it is hardly necessary to point out their extraordinary power to attract or repel, to liberate or manipulate. Images can inspire commitment and mobilise energy. They can influence us at the conscious level and even more powerfully at the unconscious level. So in today's world, it is the image-makers who are called in to market a product or a party or a president. The seductive images in the media will write our life-scripts for us, they will tell us what life is about, what happiness means, where 'salvation' is found, what living 'with grace' involves. If we do not resist them they will begin quickly to mould the very structures of our imaginations and became the optic through which we scan reality and respond to it. To enquire about our dominant images is to enquire about what motivates our thinking and acting, what informs our worldview and our vision of life.

We raised the question above (page 36) about the possible opposition between these dominant images and those which we claim to be at the heart of our Christian spirituality. In this chapter, however, we will be concerned with the images, metaphors and models that have been used down through the centuries to speak about grace and salvation. We will be wondering about the adequacy and appropriateness of these images and models, about the effect they might have had on Christian living and liturgy. But we will begin simply by recognising the existence and influence of such images in our own lives.

Our struggle to live as disciples of Jesus Christ is sustained by a theology and a spirituality which in turn are articulations of a dominant image of him and of what salvation in him means. When we are asked why we are Christians, or why we do certain things, as Christians, we usually respond by holding our dominant image of Christ our saviour before our mind's eye, reading off certain of that images characteristics and saying: 'I am like this because he is ....' The very structure of that statement makes us aware of the extent to which that master-image influences us, draws forth and organises our energy and patterns our response.

That image may be very complex indeed and each of us will
have our own story of how it developed or was modified or was
radically changed. A whole set of influences from personal experience, family, church, school, folklore, art-forms and prayer
probably went into its construction. In that image is the seed of
our thinking and acting as Christians, the code that conditions
what we do or say.

Metaphor and models
It is vitally important to be aware of the origin and development
of the images we have of grace and salvation, but theologians[1]
also alert us to the complex ways in which images function within religious language and tradition. They point out that because
their subject is mystery, there can never be a simple one-to-one
correspondence between the images used and the reality signified. What is affirmed theologically can never correspond exactly
to God, Christ, grace or salvation; it will always be improper
and inappropriate. This is why metaphor is so important, for it is
an image or a word or a phrase used inappropriately. Metaphor
is usually defined as 'the transposition of an alien name' or 'the
deliberate yoking of opposites', so we are challenged to see the
connectedness of realities previously unrelated in our minds
and imaginations. It gives us, as James Joyce put it, 'two thinks
at a time'. The disjunction, the impropriety of what is brought
together and is affirmed in metaphor should elicit, as its proper
response, 'it is not'! But because the 'is' has been affirmed, a
dialectical process is set up which opens up new insights and offers a glimpse of a new reality. Sally McFague sees metaphors as
'imaginative leaps across a distance – the best metaphors always
giving a shock and a shock of recognition.' (1987, p 35) Because
she is convinced that 'belief is related to an imaginative and
credible picture ... of the relationship between God and the
world' she insists on 'metaphor as unsubstitutable' in theology
and describes it as 'a strategy of desperation, not decoration.'
(1987, p 33)

A model for her is a 'metaphor with "staying power". A model
is a metaphor that has gained sufficient stability and scope so as
to present a pattern for relatively comprehensive and coherent
explanation.' (1987, p 34) They can help to select, organise, structure, interpret, thematise, simplify and unify complex data.

Perhaps as you read through the rich and diverse scriptural material in the previous chapter you wished that there were some definition or theory or dominant image or metaphor to draw it all together and explain its interconnectedness. Such a dominant metaphor would be a model. The plurality of models in the Christian tradition are ways of attending to the 'root-metaphor' (Stephen Pepper, *Word Hypotheses*, 1942) of Christianity itself. That root-metaphor is the relationship between God and human beings exemplified in Jesus Christ. It qualifies as metaphor because it is 'a tensive relationship distinguished by trust in God's impossible way of love, in contrast to the loveless ways of the world.' (1982, p 108) Theological models attempt to structure and re-structure that root-metaphor by drawing together the manifold subsidiary metaphors of scripture and tradition in new ways so as to illuminate what is most significant in it.

This is how McFague summarises the use of models in theology: 'The central role of models in theology is to provide grids or screens for interpreting this relationship between the divine and human. Theological models are dominant metaphors with systematic, comprehensive potential for understanding the many facets of this relationship. Metaphors could not do this alone, for the relationship is a network or structure with too many intricate implications .... Concepts could not do this alone, for the relationship is too complex, rich and multivalent for univocal concepts to define; it needs the simplifications of complementary metaphors with their expansive detail to intimate this relationship. The attitudinal and behavioural influence of metaphors (which abstract concepts never have) is needed as well in order to express the power of this transforming relationship. Thus metaphorical and conceptual language must participate in interpreting this relationship and we see this process occurring in a unique way in models.' (1982, p 125)

Finally we must remember that even the most powerful, dominant models are always time-conditioned and culturally-conditioned. If we forget this, there is a real danger that they may be used in ways which exclude complementary models or that they become 'sacralised' and therefore unquestionable or, quite simply, ossified.

An example

Perhaps at this stage an example might help to draw together the material from the preceding paragraphs and lead us into the

subject matter of the rest of the chapter. Very soon after I began
primary school, I overheard the catechism answer which explained why Jesus Christ had to die. 'Heaven was shut against
mankind by the sin of Adam and could not be opened except by
the death of Christ.' Heaven, everyone knew, had a golden gate
and St Peter was the gatekeeper and I could see it and hear it
banging shut when Adam and Eve ate the 'forbidden fruit'. The
catechism made it clear that it could not be re-opened by anyone
except Christ and not even Christ but Christ by his death. Those
awesome, mesmerising images of a shut gate and a dead Christ,
which united heaven and earth, burgeoned in my imagination
as a child. Being without competition at that formative stage,
they immediately dominated my imaginative world and became the fundamental images which explained everything else.
This was the awful consequence of sin; this was what Calvary
meant; this was why we offered the Holy Sacrifice of the Mass;
this was why we made the Stations of the Cross, prayed the sorrowful mysteries of the Rosary and abstained from meat on
Fridays; this was what grace and salvation really meant.

That compound image was so total and complete that it was
quite unquestionable and it assimilated all other images to itself
by subordination. (In retrospect, I could see that it had become a
very powerful model.) Any attempt by teachers during my
teenage years to explain something called 'satisfaction' seemed
quite redundant and to be seeking gratuitously to complicate
my preferred approach. Even a first brush with formal theology
did not force any reconsideration of that familiar model and at
most added a few footnotes to it. It was so massively in possession in my mind and imagination that nothing I learnt about the
different positions of different authors was strong enough to
dislodge it from its dominant position or bring about its decon-
struction. It was several years later before I was able to scan the
history of soteriology and discern there a substantial number of
quite distinct models that sought to communicate the significance for salvation of the life, death and resurrection of Jesus
Christ. For example, scholars point to ten models used by St
Paul to speak about distinctive aspects of the mystery of Christ's
saving work – justification, salvation, reconciliation, expiation,
redemption, freedom, sanctification, transformation, new creation
and glorification. From other parts of the New Testament we
meet such models as new birth, gift of the spirit, fellowship of

life with God through Christ, filial knowledge, illumination, in-
dwelling etc, etc. In the Christian centuries, choices were made
out of this extraordinary plurality of models which led to an impoverishment of that tradition, but others, as we will see, were
added to the number.

It was both fascinating and liberating to discover that what I had
accepted as a single model was in fact an attempted synthesis of
many models. But it was also shocking to realise that some com-
ponents of that model were taken from other models which
would be difficult to reconcile with the Judaeo-Christian tradition!

Testing our models
I believe that all of us interpret the root-metaphor of Christianity
in terms of some dominant model or other, in ways that are similar to what I have just outlined. This model then becomes so
familiar to us that we use it spontaneously as an interpretative
key to the reality of grace and salvation, but also to understand
the Christian community and its mission and role in the world.
We may be inclined to doubt the existence of any viable alternative to that model, but at some level we must admit that no
model or collection of models can ever measure up to the fullness of the mystery itself. This admission should mean that we
would be prepared to enquire about the adequacy of our preferred model, about its fidelity to what the scriptures tell us
about God's saving love in history and its climax in Jesus Christ.
We might wonder too about the coherence and the consistency
of that model and how it is related to what actually happens in
our lives. Should we not be prepared then, to test out our
favoured model against what we have already recovered from
the scriptures and against what can be retrieved from the
Christian tradition? This is no easy undertaking, as we might be
left wondering if God or Christ would recognise what they have
been doing, in the models we have formed of what we think
they have been doing!

This testing of our preferred model is absolutely essential because the Catholic tradition has always maintained that the
liturgy is about grace and salvation. But while we affirm that,
we must ask: Do the models of grace and salvation out of which
we celebrate the liturgy measure up as fully as possible to what
God seeks to communicate to us through the memorial of

Christ's life, death and resurrection? Is there a danger that we might be fitting the liturgy into our received or preferred models of grace and salvation, and thereby diminishing it or distorting it? To take an extreme example: If our dominant model is that of propitiation, we could not but distort the liturgy.

I will endeavour to outline some of the more significant ways in which theologians and Christian teachers have spoken of grace and salvation down through the centuries. Christians have always been convinced about the saving significance of Christ's life, death and resurrection, but no single model or expression of that significance has ever gained universal acceptance. This presentation of comparative positions and counter-positions should help us to identify the sources of our own models and provide us with the opportunity to decide about their present adequacy and future feasibility. I will refer to these positions as 'models' for ease of reference, and not because I believe that every characteristic of theological models is verified in each case.

1. The divinisation/participation model
It is difficult to enter into conversation with the writings of the Fathers of the early church. The cultural assumptions of their worldview, their ways of interpreting scripture, their lack of an historical sense, their anthropological viewpoint, may seem unfamiliar or even strange to many of us. If we approach their writings expecting to find a continuation of the work of the New Testament authors, or a development of what we might regard as their more promising models, or a generally acceptable explanation of the meaning of the life, death and resurrection of Jesus Christ, we will be disappointed. They select rather than synthesise, affirm rather than explain, symbolise rather than systematise, assume rather than give reasons. And out of the plethora of New Testament models, they chose for elaboration, almost exclusively, the model of ransom/redemption.

It should help us to be more sympathetic to what we find in their writings if we keep in mind the challenges and the threats that faced them. The challenges came from the demands of proclamation in the Eastern and Western milieux. In a pagan world obsessed by manifold insecurities, and where people sought 'salvation' in many conflicting forms, these teachers had to communicate the Christian conviction about the reality of salvation in Jesus Christ alone. They had to endeavour to do so in ways that took account of the preoccupation of their hearers, and be intelligible and persuasive in terms of their cultural and religious backgrounds. So they would have to address Christianity's 'cultured despisers', sophisticated sympathisers, and the ordinary uneducated people.

The threats came in two forms – gnosticism (and later Manichaeism) and the doctrinal disputes within the church itself. (Not all these Fathers are wrestling with gnosticism as such but their struggle is often with kindred difficulties.) Gnosticism claimed to offer a solution to the problem of evil and promised salvation through special knowledge (*gnosis*) communicated by a redeemer who descended from heaven to gather the elect (the rest could not be saved). They accepted a dualism of a good God beyond the cosmos and a demonic demiurge who created the cosmos and was the source of evil. Consequently they despised the material world and disparaged the human body as the entrapment of divine light. Against them, these teachers affirmed that there is only one creator God and that God's creation is good and that humanity is created in the image and likeness of God. Consistent with their basic dualism, the gnostics also rejected the incarnation, Christ's atoning death and bodily resurrection. Against these positions, these patristic authors affirmed the integrity of his humanity and the slavific character of his death and resurrection. But where we might expect an extended treatment of these topics to strengthen their case, we find that they are much more preoccupied with Jesus Christ as the lawgiver, teacher, the bestower of true knowledge and immortality.

Against the determinism and fatalism of the gnostics, these teachers replied that, while human beings were far from God's creative design for them, responsibility for that situation lay in human freedom and not with God the creator. Here they invoke the story of Adam and Eve, literally understood for the most part, and assuming a corporate solidarity of all humanity in them. They use this story, so interpreted, to shed light on the present sad plight of human beings, although they differ substantially in their assessment of the injury done to the human race by 'the fall'. This depiction of the human condition tends to be more pessimistic in the West than in the East. But even those who postulate that it had catastrophic consequences for all human beings in terms of death and corruption, never suggest that there was any transmission of guilt from Adam and Eve to their descendants.

The other threat to unity came from the trinitarian and christo-logical disputes of the fourth and fifth centuries, which were concerned ultimately with the reality of God's graciousness and salvation in Jesus Christ. It was crucial for them to maintain that in the God of Jesus Christ alone was salvation to be found. And in turn it became indispensable to say who or what Jesus Christ was in himself, if they were to continue to maintain their convic-tion about the uniqueness of what God had done and was con-tinuing to do through him. Soteriological concern was the driv-ing force of their christology. Indeed during those internecine struggles, the soteriological principle, 'what was not assumed was not healed' was the basic, and often the only guideline to distinguish between orthodoxy and heterodoxy.

When we enquire how the work of Christ as grace and salvation was understood, we notice two main currents in patristic thought. One could be called Pauline and is more typical of the West. Its restrained optimism stresses the forgiveness of sin and the restoration in Christ of what was lost in Adam. Ransom/re-demption is its preferred model and it emphasises our participa-tion in the Paschal mystery of Christ – especially through suffer-ing – in the hope of exchatological resurrection.

The other stream may be called Johannine and it is characterised by optimism. It rehearses the themes of grace as life and love and of human beings as sharers in eternal life already. Here the emphasis is not merely on restoration but on transforming union with God. The dominant model is undoubtedly that of di-vinisation. Perhaps the ever presence of neo-Platonism in that world, with its stress on the kinship between the soul and the divine, helped in opening up that prospect of divinisation. Or perhaps their long battles with pessimistic gnosticism was a cat-alyst in the process. Be that as it may, they could appeal to an in-disputable basis in scripture for their conviction. The text, 2 Pet 1:3-4 (see above p) was of crucial significance for them, as was Psalm 82:6, 'you are Gods, children of the most high, all of you' (quoted in Jn 10:34). And phrases like: 'Christ, by reason of his immeasurable love became what we are that he might make us what he himself is' (Irenaeus), or 'The Word became human so that you may learn from a human how to become divine'

(Clement of Alexandria), are repeated like mantras in their writings.

Divinisation speaks very powerfully about what must be central to any understanding of grace, namely the intimate union between God's own life and that of human beings. Yet Western theologians have always been uneasy about it, even when found in St Thomas, and have asked many questions about it. Is its use as metaphor merely a rhetorical devise? Is it a symbolic-mystical way of speaking? How does it avoid being pantheistic? Is it an example of Eastern love of paradox? Does it obscure the distinction between creature and creator? If you are born human and in time, is it not too late to be divine and eternal? No doubt, for the East, these are inappropriate questions and the influence of the model of divinisation is manifest in the divine liturgy.

2. The transactional model or Christus Victor

Many people who lived during the early centuries of the common era believed themselves to be beset by malevolent, praeternatural forces and they experienced a morbid fear and anxiety in the face of the brutal contingency of life. Their tendency to see misfortune and suffering as punishment for wrong-doing made that situation even more intolerable. Gnosticism drew on the image of 'warfare' familiar to them in life and song and story to explain that the conflicts and antagonisms of daily life in this demon-ruled world, were but pale shadows of the cosmic warfare being waged between the forces of good and evil. The victorious outcome was assured and the elect could share in it through saving knowledge.

Christians living in that same milieu also drew on the image of warfare in their teaching and catechesis about salvation, and they proclaimed that Christ had confronted all evil and overcome it definitively. They could offer strong warrant for these images of warfare and the victorious hero. It was to be found in the battle images of the First Testament and Apocalyptic. Jesus was presented in the synoptics as confronting the evil one and 'binding the strong man'. From Pauline tradition they could garner references to Christ's overcoming the tyranny of the law and sin and death thereby releasing human beings from bondage; to the 'victory given us through our Lord Jesus Christ' (1 Cor 15:57); to 'God disarmed the principalities and powers and made a public example of them, triumphing over them in him'

(Col 2:15); to our own struggle being 'against principalities and powers, against the world rulers of this present darkness, against the spiritual hosts of wickedness in the heavenly places' (Eph 6:12). They could draw on the Johannine dichotomies and the references to the 'Prince of this world' and finally to the imagery of the Apocalypse, especially chapter twelve.

From all this they composed the Drama of Redemption (as this model is sometimes called) in which Christ as warrior-hero confronts all evil and wins the definitive victory over the devil. A rudimentary version of this is found in Justin the Apologist (c.165) – because they violated God's law all human beings were under a curse and the demons were to blame. The aim of the incarnation was the conquest of the serpent and the fallen angels who imitated his example and the 'crucifixion shattered the might of the serpent who instigated Adam's transgression'. In Irenaeus (c.180) the storyline is much more sophisticated and God's approach very courteous!: '... he gave himself as a ransom for those who were led into captivity. And since the devil unjustly ruled over us by an apostasy and whereas we by nature belonged to Almighty God, alienated us contrary to nature, making us his own disciples, he, the Word of God, powerful in all things, and not failing in his own justice, behaved justly even as against the very apostasy; redeeming what was his own from that apostasy, not violently (or abitrarily) ... not insatiably seizing on what was his own but by way of persuasion ... and not by employing violence; so that neither should the law of justice be violated nor the ancient creation of God perish.' (A.H. 5, 1.1)

In this version, God is presented as recognising the 'rights' of the devil so the only possibility of deliverance for human beings would be if the devil did not abide by the rules. And of course he did not. In Gregory of Nyssa's version, the devil transacts a bargain with God whereby he will surrender all those over whom he has dominion if he can gain possession of Jesus of Nazareth whose unique virtue he has recognised but whose divinity he has not discerned. Gregory compares the human flesh of Christ to bait on the hook of his divinity. The death of Jesus is seen as the final onslaught of the devil and the demonic forces against him but, because he is the sinless Son of God, the devil can never lay claim to him. So the devil is fooled and defeated and human beings are set free.

Many other writers took up and elaborated on that image of bait and hook, adding other images like the bird-net or mouse-trap (Augustine). A few, like Gregory Nazianzen, rejected the entire model. Today we may feel like either laughing or crying when we come across these bizarre images. Indeed we may feel deeply uncomfortable with the basic transactional model itself. We may wonder about its portrayal of God, its understanding of 'justice' and God's respecting malign power and trickery, its attribution of such power to the devil that it sails close to dualism. At another level we may question the usefulness of invoking the figure of the devil to deal with the problem of evil – because he too was created and the problem goes back to God anyway. Or we may wonder how (trickery aside) it sheds any light on how the human race is saved. Or speculate about the effect of this model on popular religiosity and the celebration of liturgy. Or wonder how grace or graciousness could be said to characterise the God of this model. Yet for all our reserve, we must accept that this model achieved well-nigh universal acceptance in East and West until the advent of Anselm's satisfaction model. (Gustaf Aulen in his book, *Christus Victor* (1931), even claimed that it was the classic view, the most common approach throughout Christian history). And long afterwards it continued to influence and fascinate the imagination of other generations and found a powerful exponent in Martin Luther. The popularity of the legend of the 'Harrowing of Hell' in the art and drama of the middle ages bears witness to its continued currency.

3. The expiation/propitiation model

When scriptural authors use the metaphor of ransom/redemption[2] they never name the recipient of the ransom, presumably because there is none. They do not say that a ransom was paid; they hold that a debt was cancelled. It is a metaphor used to gain insight into God's liberation of the people, and any attempt at a literal understanding will result in a misunderstanding. In the sentences quoted above, Irenaeus mentions that the Lord redeemed us by his blood and gave himself as a ransom. Although it is found in a passage that uses the image of enslavement to the devil, it is still possible to see its meaning as being in continuity with the scriptures. With Origen this is not possible. He maintains that when St Paul asserts that we were 'bought at a price', the price in question was the blood of Christ demanded by the devil as a ransom for releasing those held in his power. (In Mt 6:8)

This is a dangerous position indeed. But he further interprets Christ's death as vicarious substitution whereby he bears our sins and suffers in our place and this sacrifice propitiates the father.

In the First Testament, by contrast, the core meaning of sacrifice[3] is that of symbolising communion of life between God and Israel. The blood, 'which is the life of the flesh' (Deut 12:23, Lev 17:11) and which 'makes atonement by reason of the life' (Lev 17:11) was understood to expiate or take away sin as we see in the ritual of purification of the mercy-seat of God on the day of atonement. (Lev 16) These rituals of sacrifice were used as powerful metaphors by New Testament authors to gain insight into the new life and communion which they experienced as coming from the life, death and resurrection of Jesus Christ. Jesus Christ is even spoken of as the new mercy-seat of God. (Rom 3:25) That use of the metaphor changed its meaning in a profound way for Christians, because the emphasis now was always on the initiative of a loving and merciful God – 'God's love for us is made manifest in that while we were yet sinners Christ died for us. (Rom 5:8) Expiation yes, propitiation no.

However, in post-New Testament times, the dividing line between expiation and propitiation was often breached and in cultural circumstances similar to those which gave rise to the previous model, Origen and many others spoke of propitiating God. This too is a contractual model for it implies some kind of negotiation and, while it is based on fear, the fear is not absolute. But such a notion takes us back beyond Christianity and beyond all but the most archaic parts of the First Testament, into contact with the savage and fickle gods of the most primitive pantheons. Yet down through the centuries, tragic and grotesque misrepresentations of Jesus' death masqueraded as Christianity and people were presented with a picture of a vampire God thirsty for blood-letting, who would only be placated by the blood of his son. The ease and frequency with which such misinterpretations recur and gain support show us that religious 'sophistication' is a fragile victory.

An honest appraisal of our own complex religious experiences may help us understand the recurrence of this model. The whole set of images through which we try to express the mystery of the God of Jesus Christ are always available to us and at times we may revert to earlier and more primitive understandings. The symbolism of blood speaks to us at a profound and primordial level and envokes an ambivalent response in us. The temptation to find the source of misfortune and suffering in divine punishment for wrongdoing is strong in many of us and we may feel drawn to appease the offended one. We may at times employ the metaphors of 'stain' or 'contamination' to understand the reality of sin and, if we do, expiation will also appeal to us. At other times awareness of the shadow side of ourselves and others may tempt us to believe in the even darker shadows represented by propitiation. Yet the disturbing questions remain: Can propitiation be a model of salvation in any credible sense? How could its God be described as gracious? And finally what damage would the expousal of such a model do to the celebration of the memorial of Jesus Christ?

4. The Augustinian/Pelagian models

It is impossible within a few paragraphs to offer even a brief sketch of the opposing positions of Augustine and Pelagius. At most we can only hint at a few central issues in the acrimonious debate between them. Augustine, like Paul, was a convert and, if we do not keep that in mind constantly, we will misunderstand his writings. His spiritual odyssey led him through youthful disillusionment with Christianity to a nine-year involvement with dualistic Manichaeism. That was followed by a period of profound scepticism which gave way to a deep attachment to Platonism. Finally, after a long crisis and painful indecision, he accepted Christianity in 384, was baptised and decided to become a monk. It was truly 'a lingering-out sweet skill'. (Hopkins)

His writings, which earned him the title Doctor of Grace, might be described as a most profound and lyrical commentary, quarried from his own experience, on the biblical notions of *hanan*, *hesed*, *charis*. He speaks of grace, God's loving kindness, as illumination, as knowledge of God, as rebirth, as justification, as participation in the divine nature (the mystery of the 'exchange of natures'), as divinisation ('The word became what we are that we might become what we are not. To make humans Gods, God became human.') (Sermo, 117) He maintains that there is the closest relationship imaginable between Christ and the Christian, a union in love which is the gift of the Holy Spirit.

'God's love has been poured into our hearts through the Holy Spirit who has been given to us' (Rom 5:5) was probably his favourite text. He never tires of speaking of this new transforming energy of love that is poured out by the spirit which enables us to love both the gift we have been given and the Giver. It is only those who love at some level who can begin to appreciate the sublime quality of this love. 'Show me a lover,' he cries, 'and s/he feels what I am saying.' (In Jn 26) He declares 'my weight is my love and wheresoever I am carried it is by that I am carried.' (Conf 13:9) He sees conversion as 'being drawn by delight' into sharing in the liberating energy and life of the lover. Of the God who is 'more intimate to me than I am to myself' he can say: 'Because you have loved me you have made me lovable.' In the light of these convictions he can tell his hearers: 'In order then to love God, let God dwell in you, and let him love himself through you.' (Sermo 1:8) The supreme summary of his theology of grace is 'Love and do what you will.' (In Jn 7)

Between 397-401, he wrote his *Confessions* in which he reviews his entire life under the rubric of profound gratitude for the gracious love and mercy of God. It remains a classic document for any experiential understanding of grace. When he recalls the final moment of his conversion, he grapples with the painful paradox of the liberty and bondage of the human will which he had experienced so acutely. In the letter to the Romans (which Augustine had studied prior to his conversion), St Paul gave powerful expression to the indecisiveness, contradictions and internal divisions that human beings experience in pursuit of the good: 'I can will what is right, but I cannot do it.' (7:18) Augustine had found this verified at the deepest level within himself. He notes how his body 'more easily obeyed the slightest will of my soul ... than my soul obeyed itself in carrying out its own strong will, for which nothing was needed except the will.' (C.8) After his conversion he believed that he now was capable of doing what he might have willed previously but could never do. He was convinced that such a breakthrough did not come from himself but was actualised in him by the grace of God independently of any prior consent of his will. His prayer became: 'Give what you command and command what you will.' When a man named Pelagius heard a bishop quote this prayer, he became angry and was sacandalised because it seemed to deny human freedom and self-determination and encourage passivity and fatalism.

Pelagius arrived in Rome sometime after 384 and soon became a popular spiritual director. He was appalled by the moral laxity of Christians in the Imperial City and was strongly opposed to Manichaeism. Christianity, he believed, was about newness of life and should make a difference to daily living. Christians should be distinguishable from pagans, and by their lives should be a sacrament of God's grace in the world. Accordingly he began to propose a robust form of Christian living to his hearers which encouraged asceticism and was intolerant of any excuses for refusing to pursue perfection. 'Be perfect as your heavenly father is perfect' (Mt 5:48) was his key text and he was convinced that God would not command the impossible. It would be non-sense to speak about virtue if it did not imply freedom of choice. 'God willed that men and women carry out this righteousness voluntarily. For this reason he left them in the hands of their own free will; and he placed before them life and death, good and evil. Whichever they would choose would be given to them ... If we do good we do it voluntarily, and the same holds true if we do evil. We will always be free to choose one of the two, and both are equally in our power.' (Letter to Demetrias)

Against the Manichees, he maintained that creation itself was 'very good' and that in creating human beings God had given them the inestimable gift of free will. Free will he saw as the prim-ary grace but he also acknowledged the law of Moses, the gospel and example of Jesus Christ, and the forgiveness of sin that came through his death and resurrection, as mediations of God's grace. God gives human beings the basic capacity to choose freely but the choosing and acting on that choice depend on their freedom. They are responsible, and if they choose they can keep the commandments and lead holy and sinless lives. And they are accountable to God who rewards and punishes. Rightdoing or wrongdoing was a matter of clear, conscious, free acts.

Pelagius believed that physical and spiritual death followed on Adams' sin, that he was a bad example to the race, that we are surrounded by a sinful environment and that most people add to it in their turn. But he denied that all sinned in Adam; that his guilt was passed on by physical descent; that sin had entered and distorted our nature independently of our choices; that our free-will was not intact. In keeping with the position of many other teachers, he taught that baptism effected the remission of sins for adults but, in the case of infants, since they had no sin, it brought initiation into the kingdom, sanctification, illumination and adoption as children of God. It was this teaching in particular that brought him to Augustine's attention.

From his *Retractions*, written shortly before his death, we know that Augustine had once thought that the first steps towards faith and conversion could be made by drawing on one's own resources. Even in 395 he could write, 'it is up to us to will or believe; it is up to God to grant those willing and believing the power of good action through the Holy Spirit'. Pelagius would find no fault with that. But by 397 it is the total dependence on God during all stages, from turning to God to union with God, that is being stressed. Everything is totally gratuitous. God's prevenient grace is active long before the will assents to the good. This grace actually brings about the assent and consequent co-operation. Humankind is now seen as a 'lump of perdition', and if individuals receive the grace of faith it can only be because God chooses them without their prior consent and without reference to their past or future good works. Those not chosen for this grace are justly condemned. This is a very dangerous position, which unfortunately will become more extreme as he takes up the cudgels against Pelagius and his supporters. Against the Pelagian conviction that as creatures with free-will we need only the guidance of Christ's teaching and our own resolve to fulfil it, Augustine paints a gloomy picture of human sinfulness and the bondage of human will without grace. Despite his unsurpassable appreciation of symbols, he reduces the total language of the powerfully symbolic story of Adam and Eve to the level of theoretical explanation and presents them as sinning heinously, and declares that all humankind were in them 'as in a root'. Everyone inherits both the guilt and the disasterous consequences of that sin. The practice of infant baptism, he held, shows that all are infected by that sin. Unbaptised children would be punished eternally in the 'mildest sufferings of hell'! As 'a mass of perdition', humankind is in bondage from within to sin, unable to use the gift of free-will to choose the good. We need grace, not as an external aid so that we may choose and act more easily as Pelagius taught, but as an interior assistance which transforms the heart of our freedom. He distinguishes between free-will and true freedom (liberty). We may indeed choose freely but what we choose may be destructive for ourselves and others because of the distortions within us. We are truly free when God's grace so suffuses our wills that we spontaneously yet freely choose the transcendent good in all our choices, and ultimately the one in whom our 'restless hearts' find rest – 'Receiving the Holy Spirit through whom there comes to be in his mind, the delight in and love of that supreme and unchangeable good which is God.' (De Sp.3) Finally, all the glory must be referred to God for the human person cannot merit, 'in crowning our merits, God is crowning God's own gifts'. (Letter 194)

Augustine and Palagius were working with radically different images of the relatedness of God's grace and human freedom within the process of salvation. But those dominant images had serious implications too for all models of creation, revelation, faith, of the Christian vision of existence, of good and evil and even of God. We may find fault with the extrinsicism of Pelagius' understanding of grace, or take issue with his individualism, eletism, and synergism, which failed to take account of human solidarity in both sin and salvation, or we may question his humanoid version of freedom but what he was trying to say deserved a much fairer hearing than it received. We may applaud Augustine's brilliant insights, profound analysis and trenchant defence of the gratuitousness of grace, but we must recognise that some of his 'defence' of these crucial issues has left us with a fearful legacy. That legacy became permanent when moderate Augustinianism became accepted as the teaching of the Church.

In the bible, the primary emphasis is ineluctably on salvation, and sin is the shadow that highlights the undeserved graciousness of God's loving initiative, 'grace abounded all the more'. Augustine reversed that order completely so that sin predominates. In addition, his understanding of double predestination and his non-universalist presentation of salvation seem impossible to reconcile with the God of Jesus Christ or his own earlier eulogising of the graciousness of that God. His teaching on the transmission of guilt from Adam, his version of the link between original sin and baptism, his consigning of unbaptised infants to hell, his pessimistic anthropology, and his denegration of human sexuality have continued to haunt the West. Pelagius may have lost in the ecclesiastical councils and Augustine may have won but the central issues of this controversy are perennial. A participant may bring to the celebration of liturgy, convictions, attitudes and outlook that are influenced by both the Augustinian and Pelagian positions!

5. The satisfaction model of St Anselm (1033-1109)

Most of us have been exposed to a version of this model, which for eight-hundred years has dominated Roman Catholic think-ing about the meaning of salvation in Jesus Christ. In developing the satisfaction model, Anselm seems to have drawn on his ex-periences of the feudal system, monastic life and the church's penitential system. Taken on its own terms, it is an excellent ex-ample of astute catechetical inculturation. However its language and concepts are of necessity, socially, culturally and historically conditioned and its key notions – honour, justice, satisfaction, merit – were liable to be misunderstood at another time and in another place. Anselm resolutely opposed the dominant model of the time (no 2) which pictured salvation as ransoming the human race from the devil ('The devil has no justice on his side against humankind' he said). Yet through a tragic misrepresent-ation of his approach, many Christians came to believe that 'sat-isfaction' meant appeasing an angry, shylock-God, jealously protective of divine honour, demanding the last ounce and last drop, demanding the death of the only son in reparation for the injustice of Adam's sin.

To understand what he actually intended, we need to recall the sense of solidarity that existed between vassals and lords within feudalism. Honour was not a personal attribute of the lord; in-stead it was a quality of his role as guarantor of public order, peace and freedom within that contractual system. Any in-fringement of honour, in this sense, brought the threat of lawlessness and chaos to all members of society. Honour would then have to be restored through satisfaction or reparation which surpassed the injury done by the offence. This was done not just to appease the offended lord, but to restore public order and peace for and behalf of all.

When Anselm applies these notions of satisfaction and honour to human-divine relations, he is well aware of their metaphoric nature. Human beings were created for obedience and service to God, but right relations between God and human beings have been perverted by sin. God has been dis-honoured and therefore the whole order and beauty that God intended, was in jeopardy. It was justice, not God, that demanded that God's honour be restored. This infinite offence (since the criterion refers to the one offended) cannot simply be overlooked by God since it involves not only God but the entire order of things, and so reparation cannot bypass but must involve free human beings. 'It is not fitting for God to do anything unjustly or without due order; it does not belong to his freedom or kindness or will to forgive unpunished the sinner who does not repay to God what s/he took away'. Within these parameters order could only be restored if someone were to make satisfaction which would be greater than the offence. Human beings should make satisfaction to excess but they cannot (they already owe everything that could be offered to God and at any rate , could never offer anything infinite); God could make that satisfaction but may not. 'None but true God can make it, none but true man owes it.' This dilemma is resolved by the offering of Jesus Christ the God/man. (This also is the answer to the question in the title of his work, *Cur Deus Homo?* / Why the incarnation?) Because he is sinless, he is not subject to death but when he freely offers himself in death this 'excess' merits a reward which he does not need and which God in mercy then passes on to human beings. In this way he restores harmony to the world and honour to God and introduces a new order of peace and freedom.

Anselm believed that he could present a simple and lucid argument for the necessity of the incarnation and the cross. He did not intend it to depend on scriptural details but the resonances of many scriptural themes can be heard throughout the work. His understanding of justice, too, is biblical rather than juridical and is basically a synonym for holiness and mercy. (Later it will be heard only as juridical.) Against the passivity induced by the transactional model, he sought to open up a more relational understanding of the divine/human drama and emphasise freedom and obedience. And it has had a profound influence on scholars and non-scholars alike and it found a powerful champion in Martin Luther.[4]

Yet even on its own terms (in so far as they are recoverable), it has its weaknesses: it is painfully cerebral and rationalistic in its approach to something as mysterious as God's 'impossible way of love' – How can you 'prove' the 'necessity' of the incarnation?

It seems to accept that the incarnation was initiated as a response to sin rather than as being part of God's eternal design. It doggedly follows its own logic in relation to the cross and ignores the resurrection and indeed the significance of Christ's life and ministry. It opposes the contractual model yet it is basically about a negotiation between Jesus Christ and God, and human beings are once again relegated to being onlookers at what has been achieved 'objectively'. Of course it was not taken on its own terms, and we can only guess at the catastrophic consequences of the misrepresentations of the satisfaction model for liturgical celebrations for countless Christians during eight centuries.

6. Abelard's model

Peter Abelard (died 1142) also rejected any suggestion that humanity had been ransomed from the devil, but he did not support the newly-formulated teaching of Anselm either. The idea of the devil obtaining 'rights' as a result of successful temptation seemed absurd to him, and he had no desire either to treat Christ's work as a logical necessity, for God, he believed, could easily have forgiven human beings. He recoiled from the thought that 'God would find pleasure in the death of his Son in order that he might thereby be reconciled to the world'. Both the contractual and the Anselmian models left human beings as involved spectators at (but somehow later beneficiaries of) heavenly or cosmic happenings and did not explain how 'objective' and 'subjective' redemption were related.

Abelard did not believe that the focus should be on any external payment or reparation, so by contrast he emphasised the interiority of both the human malady and its cure through Christ. His diagnosis of the human predicament was that it derived from lovelessness rather than disorder and lawlessness, and so the remedy would have to be an act of love. This Johannine emphasis on love and its power to transform those who love, pervades his entire presentation – 'greater love no one has ...' (Jn 15:13) was his key text. 'I think ... that the purpose and cause of the incarnation was that he might illuminate the world by his wisdom and excite it to love of himself.' Again he says, 'we have been justified by the grace of him – that is God – who first loved us ... through this unique act of grace manifested to us – in that his Son has taken upon himself our nature and persevered therein in teaching us by word and example even unto death – he has more fully bound himself to us in love; with the result that our hearts should be enkindled by such a gift of divine grace, and through charity should not shrink from enduring anything for him'. This conviction that salvation takes place through the power of Jesus Christ's love and teaching and example to turn human beings away from sin, is reinforced by other much quoted lines from his *Exposition on Romans*: 'Our redemption is that supreme love which is in us through the passion of Christ, that love that not only frees us from slavery to sin, but also wins for us the true liberty of God's children, so that we do all things out of love rather than fear.'

The cross of Christ was not just an example for human beings; it was for Abelard, as for Paul, proclamation. It was the manifestation of the weakness of love, of the extent to which God was prepared to go in identifying with us. And the resurrection was the manifestation of the power of love. Our lovelessness led to the cross where the suffering love of God was revealed, but in the resurrection, in the victory of the strength of weakness, love was revealed as life.

Through Christ human beings are a new creation, but this must be seen in terms of new possibilities of love and liberation from sin. When we discover the boundless love of God and realise that we were loved even when we were sinners, we should begin to love in return and no longer wish to sin. And because we see Jesus Christ being loved by God, even in the negativities of suffering and death, in what constitutes the supreme fear and dread for human beings, we can believe in and respond to that same love even in our own most negative experiences.

Abelard's model is very close to what the gospels tell us about the life and death of Jesus Christ and to the best of what Augustine had to say, especially on the exemplary aspect of Christ's work ('nothing is greater in eliciting love than prevenient love'). But it was so different from the thinking current at that time that it was rejected and he was accused of Pelagianism by Bernard of Clairvaux. (The fact that he saw through and pointed to the contradictory nature of the Augustinian theology of original sin as inherited guilt – the only one to do so for fourteen hundred years – did not help his cause!) His stress on the personal and relational would be rejected as subjectivist and exemplarist in later centuries, when the dominant categories were the juridic and the ontological. He was 'rediscovered' by liberal Protestants in the nineteenth century but perhaps it is only in recent times that his position can be fairly assessed. Consequently we cannot assess the influence of this model on liturgy.

7. The nature/supernature model

We have seen already how easily the abundance of New Testament models could be forgotten and a single model predominate. Against that tendency, Thomas Aquinas rehabilitated some of the complex and richly varied models of grace and salvation available in scripture and tradition. He succeeded in weaving together scriptural models such as sacrifice, ransom, redemption, models taken from the Greek fathers and Anselm's satisfaction model (which he modified substantially). Yet he qualified all of them by linking them to his key concept of Christ's superabundant, liberating love. The resurrection of Jesus Christ was central to his presentation of salvation, yet he gave due weight to the saving significance of his life and death, to all aspects of the Paschal mystery and 'the mysteries of Christ's flesh'. His lasting contribution to the theology of salvation was his insistence on the salvific role of the human nature, the human will, the free, active, obedient love of Jesus Christ. In this way his work showed the relativity of all models, and we see again that no single model (or set of models) can adequately communicate the mystery of salvation.

In one of his writings, Thomas noted a change in discourse about grace, from understanding it primarily as 'God's very mercy itself' to perceiving it as 'a habitual justifying act'. (De ver. Q 24 A 14) We might summarise his own achievement by saying that he restored the primacy to God's merciful love in itself, and related to that primacy the transforming effects of that love in us. The notion of 'the supernatural' became the organising principle of his synthesis.

Philip the Chancellor (C.1225) asserted that grace was gratuitous because it was supernatural, and by that he meant that it brought human beings to a destiny that far surpassed their natural powers. Behind this statement lay the assumption that in the hierarchy of being, each one acts according to its nature and towards an end or goal proportionate to it. But the New Testament says that human beings are destined 'to be like him, for we shall see him as he is' (1 Jn 3:2) and that, already in this life, because 'God is love, whoever abides in love abides in God, and God in them' (1 Jn 4:16), for 'God's love has been poured into our hearts by the Holy Spirit who has been given to us' and they have become 'partakers of the divine nature'. (2 Pet 1:4) Yet they knew that, as creatures, God is infinitely beyond them, so that the destiny and mode of life to which they are ordained is supernatural in relation to their human nature and its powers. That destiny could only be achievable and proportionate if a further gift, a new nature so to speak, were given to human beings as grace. Grace was no longer understood to be gratuitous because of human sinfulness, as the tradition up to that time had maintained. It was now understood as gratuitous in relation to human nature itself, which it heals and elevates and makes proportionate to life with God, as goal.

For our purposes here, there is no need to examine the comprehensive and subtle use that St Thomas made of that unity-in-distinction of natural/supernatural to show how grace, as the bestowal of God's own self, corresponds to the deepest longings of the human spirit and yet is absolutely gratuitous. This is not because that distinction is not important but because very soon it was misunderstood and, at the hands of others, it became separation. Cajetan (1468-1534) misunderstood radically what Thomas had said about the natural desire for the vision of God, and concluded that human beings had both a natural last end (philosophic contemplation of God) and a supernatural end to which God gratuitously called them. Within fifty years, theologians were speaking about, 'state of pure nature' which was soon endowed with the natural counterparts of the gifts of grace! This dualistic approach was presented and accepted as authentic Thomistic thought and, accordingly, gained very widespread acceptance. But in it nature and supernature each constitute an integral and complete order and are not intrinsically related. (The order of nature was said to have a kind of 'potency' or non–repugnance to be elevated!) and are linked only by divine decree. This image of a two-tiered system was a kind of 'upstairs, downstairs' of the religious world. It was supposed to emphasise that grace was an absolute gift, but why should one be ecstatically grateful for something super-added to what was already complete in itself? This double-decker model defeated its own purpose, for if the supernatural were so extrinsic to

human beings, surely it could be accepted or rejected with im-
punity? And if it is spoken of in arid, technical, almost mechanical
categories, why should anyone be even interested in it?

This model is said to have given rise to indifference and to secularism, to a dualism of the sacred and the profane, to the vertical
and the horizontal, the heavenly and the earthly, the eternal and
the temporal, church and world, clergy and laity, etc., that had
disastrous consequences for christianity. These dichotomies naturally had very serious implications for the celebration of liturgy,
but when they are combined with the distorted version of the
satisfaction model, we can only guess at the negative consequences.

8. The personalist model

In 1946, Henri De Lubac published *Surnaturel*, a withering criticism of the scholastic construct, 'pure nature', which he saw as
expendable. It also contained a very strong indictment of the
theologians who propounded the natural/supernatural model
which he claimed was dualistic and extrinsic and which facilitated the growth of secularism. Karl Rahner published an essay,
'Concerning the relationship between nature and grace', in 1950
(T.I. 1, p 297ff), in which he agreed with much of what De Lubac
had said. But unlike him, he wished to retain the notion of 'pure
nature' as a 'remainder concept' to clarify the gratuitousness of
grace. In that essay he described grace as God's self-communication to humankind and to each person. He also introduced several concepts which would continue to characterise his writings
on grace: the term 'supernatural existential' as a way of speaking about the universality of grace, and the distinction between
grace 'offered' and 'accepted'. In the course of the essay he
asked: 'Could it not be said here quite rightly that it is precisely
the essence of personal being (his paradox without which he
cannot be understood) that he is ordained to personal communion with God in love (by nature), and must receive just this love
as free gift? Is this not true of earthly love too? It is ... something
to which the man giving and receiving love knows himself to be
uniquely ordained, so that he would seem lost and unhappy to
himself if he did not receive this love, and yet he accepts this
same love as the 'miracle' and the unexpected gift of free (and so
unexacted) love'. (p. 305) That final sentence may be seen as a
programmatic summary of the personalist model which gained
acceptance during the following twenty-five years.

Drawing on philosophy and psychology, a variety of authors developed a phenomenology of love and friendship which was then used to shed light on the mystery of God's graciousness. Human beings come to self-realisation in and through encounter with others. In human relationships the 'I' is intrinsically oriented towards, and is in absolute need of, the free, unforceable, gracious, self-revelation of the 'Thou', if the true self is to blossom. Yet the 'I' can scarcely hope for such an invitational revelation which alone can bring personal fulfilment. Should it happen, it can be experienced only as an entirely gracious, mysterious, undeserved and transforming gift from beyond the self, yet in delight-full harmony with the soul-cry of the self. Simultaneously, it reveals the person's real potential for intersubjectivity which had previously been experienced only as vague, unfulfilled desire.

From such an example, it is clear that the fulfilment of the goal towards which a human being is intrinsically ordered, could nevertheless be entirely gratuitous. This insight could then be applied analogically to divine-human relations to gain insight into the faith conviction, that while human beings are intrinsically ordered towards communion of life with God in grace, that it should be so is nevertheless absolutely gratuitous.

The personalist model resonates very deeply with what we have seen about grace and salvation in the scriptures. Its appeal to experience, its personal and relational language and thought categories, were very different from the dry, impersonal, technical, reified, mechanistic and metaphysical categories of the previous model. Not surprisingly, in the early years advocates of that model criticised the personalist model for having traded the ontological for the psychological, and condemned it for being subjective and exemplarist. That polarisation of positions was unfair but perhaps some presentations of the personalist model might have been more nuanced and might have paid more attention to the need for more appropriate qualifiers.

For example, if its analogical nature was not always given due recognition, the otherness of God could be forgotten, and the anthropomorphic language of the bible could be heard in a rather literal way. Even a sober theologian like Schillebeeckx could write in 1964, 'We now interact with God just as we interact with human beings, in a familiar self-disclosure and real dialogue'.[5]

God is indeed personal but God is not a person in our usual sense of the word. Furthermore the example chosen for development within this model was usually that of revelatory encounter between two adults, and that could also add to the misunderstandings. It would need to be acknowledged that in order for such self-revelation to take place each person must be already gifted by the prevenient love of others, 'the I is inhabited by others'. Perhaps the example of the prevenient love of a parent providing the total environment in which an infant can grow and develop, patiently coaxing from it the first personalising responses, encouraging its growth towards freedom (thereby risking the possibilities of later rejection), might be more appropriately applied to the grace relationship. Or again, since God cannot be available for face-to-face relationship our exploration of the powerful ways in which those who love may be personally present to each other, while being physically distant, could help. We would need to recall how the other is internalised and is present in a supportive, transforming way; how such a relationship is maintained and celebrated through symbols and lives in the hope of future face-to-face meeting. Finally it might be necessary to offset the residual individualism or selfishness which could infect this model, by recalling that love and friendship involve what may be a painful process of giving up theoretical freedom in a process of self-transcendence, in self-surrender to the other, and that ultimately it must involve developing community. The model is in deep harmony with the language of scripture and its understanding of God, and has brought a genuine enrichment to our appreciation of the divine-human relationship and its celebration in liturgy.[6]

9. The quest for meaning model
Cornelius Ernst (*The Theology of Grace*, Mercier Press, 1974) is convinced that changes in the language of grace down the centuries have always been associated with deep changes in the understanding of the relationship between God and human beings. Since we are obviously living through such a period of change, he wishes to present a perspective for a theology of grace for our time in which we could recognise our own deepest 'first hand experience.' (64) However a serious obstacle to achieving that goal is our ingrained facility for distinguishing (opposing?) 'subjective' and 'objective'. He does not believe that our experience of ourselves and our world can be adequately

analysed in terms of that distinction. And he deems it to be even more inappropriate for understanding our experience of Jesus Christ in faith and the reality of grace. In the writings of Aquinas, these categories are not applicable either, for everything is grounded in an understanding of 'being'. But today we do not readily feel at home with this primary theme of being, and he suggests that an alternative primary theme would be *meaning*. People spontaneously ask 'why'? and 'what does it mean'? in everyday language, without the aid of an abstract philosophy of meaning.[7] 'Meaning' seems to have for us today the kind of indistinct universality and obviousness which perhaps 'being' had for earlier epochs …'(67) 'Meaning' is not just a label we put on whatever we happen to like, rather it is something we discover and create within the given of reality. Ernst describes meaning as 'that praxis, that process and activity, by which the world to which man belongs becomes the world which belongs to man'.(68) Meaning is historical, 'It assumes a world prior to man into a world of human communication by work, play, dance, travel, love, conversation, reflection – the totality of human life and death, in the continuity of a humanity which inwardly transforms the biological into the historical order.' (68)

For the Christian the experience in faith of Jesus Christ, which he himself makes possible, is a new kind of understanding, a new kind of meaning, a new kind of possibility, which extends and transforms the whole process of human meaning and modifies our understanding of God and human beings. It is within this enlarged world of meaning, in this renewed web of associations, that he locates grace. In our experience of Jesus Christ in faith we are given privileged 'access to the mutual and incomprehensible mysteries of God and man in their pre-ordained union.'(66) So Jesus Christ must be the centre of any theology of grace.

Ernst sees 'destiny', God's mysterious plan for each and for all, which is raised by the question 'why'? as the form of a theology of grace. Christians believe that the answer to the 'why question' is disclosed in the destiny of Jesus Christ which is ours to share through transforming communion with him in faith, hope and love. It calls us to pass through suffering and even despair to the affirmation of praise. Its 'answer' is the way of life through death. The cross, manifesting a love in and beyond death, is its living and luminous centre. The content of a theology of grace is 'transfiguration and transformation'(72), as real as any activity of transforming the world. This newness introduced into our lives in our experience of Jesus Christ, he names as a 'genetic moment' which is manifested as self-transcending transformation of the individual life and the life of the community. This is the heart of grace and salvation.

He then reviews the questions that recur in any approach to grace, but from his chosen perspective tackles them in refreshing, illuminating ways – nature and grace, grace and freedom (explored in terms of conversion), grace and sin, grace and sacrifice, grace and the spirit.

How does he view the relationship between this quest for meaning and liturgy? In the sacraments, he believes that we can rediscover the continuity of creation, recreation and consummation, of 'nature' and grace. 'In each sacrament "nature" is assumed into a creative purpose which transcends it by being made to bear in a significant action the death and victory of Jesus, his passage into the glory of the Father. Nature, passion and glory are integrated into a comprehensive sign.'(89) The eucharist is 'not only the human behaviour of eating and drinking, a ritual doing; it is also the artefact of human meaning, something ritually made … What was bread and wine has become the embodiment of God's gracious love in the communicated flesh and blood of Jesus; what was transformed by human labour from the world to which men belonged into the world which belongs to men – wheat into bread, grapes into wine -- is now transformed into the world of God's creative love, transfigured flesh and blood.'(90)

Notes:

1. *The New Jerome Bible Commentary*, Geoffrey Chapman, 1989, 82:67-80.

2. See *Disturbing the Peace*, ch 11.

3. ibid, ch 11.

4. The Reformation models of grace and salvation are beyond the scope of this chapter.

5. *God and Man*, Sheed and Ward, 1969.

6. In the original outline of this chapter, the ninth model was intended to bring together the approaches of Process Theology, Teilhard de Chardin and Creation Theology. This seemed feasible because of the 'common element of form' (Whitehead) between their shared conviction about the priority of the category of becoming over being, their stress on the immanence of God to creation and the consequent goodness of the material world and the value of human action as co-creative. However, it became clear after several drafts, that to do justice to the uniqueness of each of these approaches would necessitate treating them as separate models. Reluctantly I decided that I should not do this as it would further extend this rather long chapter. I regret that these approaches cannot be included here, in particular, because they would have served as necessary correctives to the anthropcentricity of most of the models in this chapter. Even the model to be considered in the next chapter, liberation, suffers from that narrow focus. It has tended, so far, to concentrate almost exclusively on the world of human beings and not take the relationship between history and nature, and between the liberation of human nature and all of nature, with sufficient seriousness.

7. See 'Moments of Glad Grace' in *Disturbing the Peace*, chapter nine, in which I outline an approach to grace and salvation in terms of meaning, value and symbol.

CHAPTER 7

Liberation[1]

Hope guarantees the poor that they will be Masters at haw-time
when the robins are courageous as a crow or waterhen.
Patrick Kavanagh

I: The genesis and development of the theology of liberation

'In Latin America we don't talk about liberation theology. We talk about God and grace and sin and people. Other people call it liberation theology.' That is Jon Sobrino's attempt to good-humouredly relativise this controversial subject. It is of course passionately concerned with God and sin and grace and people but, in fact, it first received its name in Latin America in the late 1960s, and it grew out of the religious, social, political, economic and cultural circumstances that are peculiar to Latin America. The first distinctive stirrings of this (as yet anonymous) new approach are to be found on the eve of Vatican II among some of the strong student movements in the universities, which still continued to enjoy extraordinary freedom and privilege even under oppressive regimes. Here and there teachers and students sought to break through the mystifications used by governments to 'justify' the 'structures of plunder' and to expose the massive graft and injustice behind the veneer of inevitability. In most countries a minority of 5-10% controlled about 50% of the wealth, while only 5% of wealth went to the poorer 30% of the population. (For example, in Brazil in 1960, 5% of the population received 28% of the national income, rising to 39% in 1980. But during those twenty years the share going to 50% of the population had fallen from 18% to 12%).

In the early 1960s too, some students in various South American countries, already involved in Catholic Action groups, began to search for new ways of taking the social and political implications of their Christian faith more seriously. It was among such students and their chaplains, and supported by interested professional people and some theologians, that the theology of liberation had its origin. Many date its first clearly recognisable beginnings to a meeting of young Latin American theologians (including Segundo and Gutierrez) in 1964 in Petropolis, Brazil. That group were seeking ways to reflect theologically on the meaning of Christian faith in the painful and contradictory situation of their Catholic homelands. At that meeting Gutierrez described theology as 'critical reflection on praxis'.

Little beginnings
They were encouraged by the optimistic encyclicals of John XXIII, *Mater et Magistra* (1961) and *Pacem in Terris* (1963). John's own hope had been that, through the council, the church would be 'the church of all the people and in particular of the poor', but this did not become a theme of the council (despite Cardinal Lecaro's prophetic claim 'that the fundamental topic of this council is precisely the church as a church of the poor'). In establishing the identity of their new quest, the council's new approach to revelation, its new vision of the church and its mission, its declarations on religious liberty were naturally very important. In particular, *Gaudium et Spes*, which began: 'The joy and hope, the grief and anguish of the men of our time, especially of those who are poor or afflicted in any way, are the joy and the hope, the grief and anguish of the followers of Christ as well. Nothing that is genuinely human fails to find an echo in their hearts,' was to be programmatic.

While they drew on the catholicity of this new vision, they were also beginning to mould their own theological approach to the peculiarities of the local situation and to tailor their strategies to local needs. Already by 1966, people involved in this new quest were beginning to take on leadership roles within groups which met to pray, read the bible and reflect on the situations within which they lived their lives. Through this structure it was hoped to break through the apathy and fatalism that often characterises poor, oppressed people. The Basic Christian Communities were launched and began to multiply at an extraordinary rate, especially in Brazil. In what follows, I will outline the growing emphasis on liberation in ecclesial documents, returning in the second section to the theology itself.

Medellin
Pope Paul VI published his first social encyclical, *Populorum Progressio*, in 1967 which stressed the need for 'integral development' through structural change.

'Development demands bold transformations, innovations that go deep'. In the same year he set up the Pontifical Commission for Justice and Peace 'to further the progress of the poorest peoples, to encourage social justice among nations, to offer to the less developed nations the means whereby they can further their own progress'. 1968 was a black year in Latin American social and political history, but for many church people it is remembered as the year that heralded the new reformation. It is the year of Medellin.

In July of that year, in the town of Chimbote, Peru, Gustavo Gutierrez presented a paper bearing the title *Towards a theology of liberation.* The new quest had at last found its name. At Medellin, the Conference of Latin American Bishops committed the church to confront the 'institutionalised violence' of the establishment and to 'awaken in individuals and communities a living awareness of justice, to defend the rights of the poor and oppressed, and to energetically denounce the abuses and unjust consequences of the inequalities between rich and poor' ... 'The present situation ... awakens attitudes of protest and the desire for liberation, development and social justice.'

In line with this, the bishops made their famous 'preferential option for the poor'. 'The Lord's distinct commandment, 'to evangelise the poor', ought to bring us to a distribution of resources and apostolic personnel that effectively gives preference to the poorest and most needy sectors ... We the bishops wish to come closer to the poor ... We ought to sharpen the awareness of our duty of solidarity with the poor ... We make our own their problems and their struggles ... This has to be concretised in criticism of injustice and oppression, in the struggle against the intolerable situation which a poor person often has to tolerate ... We encourage those who feel themselves called to share the lot of the poor, living with them and even working with their hands ...' The bishops undertook 'to encourage and favour the efforts of the people to create and develop their own grassroots organisation for the redress and consolidation of their rights and the search for true justice'.

The ripples spread inwards
A new era of transformation in church life in Latin America, characterised by action for justice in the name of the gospel, had begun. But it was not confined to the periphery; its effects were

felt throughout church. In 1971 the apostolic letter, *Octogesima Adveniens*, underlined the fact that 'It is not enough to recall principles, state intentions, point to crying injustices, utter prophetic denunciations; these words lack weight unless accompanied ... by effective action.'

Justice in the World, the final document of the international synod held that same year, spoke of 'the serious injustices which are building up around the world of men, a network of domination, oppression and abuses which stifle freedom and which keep the greater part of humanity from sharing in the building up and enjoyment of a more just and more fraternal world.' It declared that 'action on behalf of justice and participation in the transformation of the world fully appear to us as a constitutive dimension of the preaching of the gospel, or, in other words, of the church's mission for the redemption of the human race and its liberation from every oppressive situation'. 'Liberation' had been used a few times in the Medellin documents, basically as a synonym for 'integral development.' Now it was being used in documents of the universal church. In Latin America that same year (1971) saw the publication of Gutierrez' *The Theology of Liberation*, Miranda's *Marx and the Bible*, Segundo's five-volume series *Theology for Artisans of a New Humanity* and Boff's *The Gospel of the Cosmic Christ*.

Evangelii Nuntiandi (1975) reinforced the link between action for justice and the mission of the church, between liberation and salvation. Paul VI used the term 'liberation' in the sense of 'the effort and struggle to overcome everything which condemns those people to remain on the margin of life: famine, chronic disease, illiteracy, poverty, injustices in international relations and especially in commercial exchanges, situations of economic and cultural neo-colonialism sometimes as cruel as the old political colonialism. The church is in duty bound – as her bishops have insisted – to proclaim the liberation of those hundreds of millions of people since very many of them are her children. She has a duty of helping this liberation, of bearing witness on its behalf and of assuring its full development'.

All is not quiet on the southern front

With this document we reach a kind of climax in an extraordinary movement of conscious convergence between official Roman statements and the aspirations of the episcopates and theologians of Latin America. However it would be naïve to think that a whole continent set out to translate all the documents, from Medellin to *Evangelii Nuntiandi*, into an integral way of life. Not so. But those who attempted to do so – which was, and is, a small but very significant minority – quickly incurred the wrath of those who had most to lose from such an overturning, and persecution, torture and even death followed for many. Sadly, negative reaction was not confined to the dictators. Even in the early seventies, the new wine seemed to go sour for some and, when the heady days after Medellin had passed, some local church leaders and indeed some local churches tried to undo the charter of Medellin. The shameful manipulations prior to Puebla in 1979, which sought to reverse Medellin, are unfortunately only too well known – the exclusion of theologians sympathetic to liberation, the 'packing' of delegates, the gross misrepresentations by the press, the tragic-comic posturing of so-called 'dignitaries', etc. Yet the conference, in its 'Final Document', managed to write straight, even with these very crooked lines.

It is a long and uneven document but it did re-affirm the basic vision of Medellin. In the prologue, the bishops say 'we recognise that we are still far from being all that we preach. For all our faults and limitations, we pastors ask pardon of God and our brothers and sisters in the faith.' They renew their commitment to the 'preferential option for and solidarity with the poor', adding that it is not exclusive. It goes on: 'We affirm the need for conversion on the part of the whole church, for a preferential option for the poor, an option aimed at their integral liberation.' They insist that there can be 'no evangelisation without integral liberation' and they offer a critique of 'the idols of our time' and proclaim their concern for indigenous peoples.

John Paul II, in his opening address at Puebla, declared: 'The conference now opening will have to take the Medellin conclusions as its point of departure' and reaffirmed the consensus reached under Paul VI concerning the indispensable roles of work on behalf of justice and human promotion, for evangelisation. The church, he said, teaches that 'there is a social mortgage on all private property'. In his first encyclical, *Redemptor Hominis*, published shortly after Puebla, he spoke of the 'signs of the times', of progress and growing threat, of opportunities and inequalities and disorders which called in question the status quo. His concern for the dignity of humankind made him call for a new solidarity among people and for 'daring, creative resolves' and 'the indispensable transformation of the structures of economic life.'

The confusing 80s

Likewise, in *Laborem Exercens* (1981), the Pope championed the dignity of human beings, proclaimed the primacy of labour over capital and re-affirmed the church's solidarity with the poor. The church is firmly committed to this cause 'for she considers it her mission, her service, a proof of her fidelity to Christ, so that she can truly be the church of the poor'.

After such a massive endorsement of the intrinsic relationship between the struggle for justice and the essential mission of the church by local, papal, and universal authority, one would have expected an end of opposition to the mainline liberation approach. However, the ambivalences and inconsistencies continued and received much publicity with the interrogation of Gutierrez and the silencing of Boff. 1984 became associated with 'double-think' for more than one reason!

Rumour and speculation preceded the publication of the *Instruction on certain aspects of the theology of liberation* (CDF 1984). It was feared that the Vatican was about to turn its back on the line it had been pursuing and adopt a position more in harmony with the much-publicised views of Cardinal Ratzinger. Fortunately nothing of the sort happened. While the document was indeed cautious, and in parts critical of the theology of liberation, it did state that 'the powerful and almost irristable aspiration that people have for liberation constitutes one of the principal signs of the times'. In fact it endorses the key themes of 'liberation' 'which is fundamental to the Old and New Testaments' (III, 4) and 'the church of the poor' (IX, 9; XI, 5), while warning against the abstract possibility of doctrinal deviation through the 'uncritical use of 'concepts borrowed from Marxist ideology.'

The Pope in Peru

The themes outlined so far have been taken up again and again by John Paul II on his tours of third world countries. At least one major speech on each tour has dealt with social justice, liberation, option for the poor, etc.

At Villa El Salvador, Lima, on 5 February 1985, he spoke to a huge crowd gathered from all the shanty towns around the city. Given the events of the previous year, some people were afraid he might be critical of the theology of liberation. A couple addressed him in the name of all: 'Holy Father, we are hungry, we are afflicted by poverty, we have no work, we are sick. Brokenhearted we see our wives conceive although they are stricken with tuberculosis, our infants die, our children grow up weak and without a future. But in spite of all this, we believe in the God of life, a life full of goodness and grace'. After his prepared talk, in which he stressed his solidarity with all the poor and praised those who struggled with them for freedom and justice, he said: 'I see that there is hunger for God here. This hunger is the true riches of the poor and must never be lost ... Here there is hunger for bread ... we pray 'give us this day our daily bread' for those who hunger for bread. This is necessary for Peruvian society, for the good of Peru. Daily bread must not be lacking to the young (shanty) towns (said with emphatic finger-wagging) ... it is their right ... For all these young towns, I pray that the hunger for God may remain and the hunger for bread be eliminated.'

Nevertheless, in Arequipa, Peru, in February 1985 and in Lima, January 1986, attempts were made to propose the 'theology of reconciliation' as an alternative to the theology of liberation. They were spearheaded by Cardinal Lopez Trujillo, Archbishop of Medellin, who as General Secretary of the Conference of Latin American Bishops had led the attempt at Puebla to oppose the theology of liberation. In a recent interview, he said that the 1984 CDF document had arrived too late. 'If the text had been published ten years ago, the church might have been spared much suffering, torture, martyrs and even deaths. Some theologians and many vocations might have been saved.' He went on to describe Nicaragua as 'the Vatican of liberation theology.' (See *Latin American Links*, February 1986)

The second instruction
Finally the *Instruction on Christian Freedom and Liberation* was published by CDF on 5 April 1986. It was to be read in conjunction with the 1984 instruction for 'between the two documents there exists an organic relationship'. It begins by reflecting on 'the state of freedom in the world today' and assesses the contribution of the various liberation movements. Then it discusses

'Man's vocation to freedom and the tragedy of sin', and 'Liberation and Christian freedom'. The core of the instruction is concerned with 'The liberating mission of the church' which is viewed from the perspective opened up by liberation theology. The emphasis is on the vision of the beatitudes and the power of the gospel to promote an integral liberation from everything that hinders the development of individuals. 'Hence also, those who are oppressed by poverty are the subject of a love of preference on the part of the church ... The special option for the poor, far from being a sign of particularism or sectarianism, manifests the universality of the church's being and mission. This option excludes no one.' (68) 'The new basic communities or other groups of Christians which have arisen to be witnesses to this evangelical love are a source of great hope for the church ... their experience, rooted in a commitment to the complete liberation of man, becomes a treasure for the whole church.'(69) It encouraged all theologians to take up the theme of liberation as something that was important, urgent and necessary in the life of the church (69, 70, 98). This new way of doing theology is called 'a noble ecclesial task.'

Stressing the primacy of persons over structures, it goes on: 'The recognised priority of freedom and of conversion of heart in no way eliminates the need for unjust structures to be changed. It is therefore perfectly legitimate that those who suffer oppression on the part of the wealthy or the politically powerful should take action through morally licit means in order to secure structures and institutions in which their rights will be truly respected ... It is therefore necessary to work simultaneously for the conversion of hearts and for the improvement of structures'.(75) It outlines basic principles and criteria for judging the rightness of a course of action and then says: 'These criteria must be especially applied in the extreme case where there is recourse to armed struggle, which the church's magisterium admits as a last resort to put an end to an obvious and prolonged tyranny which is gravely damaging the fundamental rights of individuals and the common good.'(79)

Speaking of the role of the laity, it reminds us once again that: 'The work of salvation is seen to be indissolubly linked to the task of improving and raising the condition of human life in this world'.(80) And it speaks of the need to work out and set in mo-

tion 'ambitious programmes aimed at the socio-economic liberation of millions of men and women caught in an intolerable situation of economic, social and political oppression'.(81) It concludes by calling for a theology of freedom and liberation which
faithfully echoes Mary's magnificat – a favourite text of theologians of liberation, who have been maintaining that God 'exalts
the lowly and fills the starving with good things'. The judgement of this document on the theology of liberation is far from
that of Lopez Trujillo.

The Pope's letter to the Brazilian bishops (9 April, 1986) was
even more explicit in its commendation of the theology of liberation: 'We are convinced that liberation theology is not only
opportune but is useful and necessary ... The poor are the first
to feel the urgent need for this gospel of radical and integral liberation. To hide it would be to cheat and disillusion them.

Summary
In Latin America during the past twenty-five years there has been
a movement away from a politically naïve and paternalistic
understanding of 'development' (as capable of ameliorating the
situation), through the more all-embracing concept of 'integral
development,' to the dawning of the importance of 'liberation'
and finally to the more nuanced understanding of 'integral liberation.' Correspondingly, the models of church have moved
from the predominantly 'hierarchical' model, through 'the church
as the People of God' (Vat II), to 'the church for the people'
(Post-Medellin) and most recently to 'the church of the people'
(Post-Puebla).

II: The principles and themes of liberation theology

I have spoken of the origins of the theology of liberation and, in
this section, I will try to outline its main principles and themes.
Although most of the better known proponents of the theology
of liberation have studied in Europe or North America, they
have reacted against some of the characteristics of first world
academic theology. All theology is concerned with an understanding of faith and all theologians must dedicate themselves
to discovering and articulating the meaning of the word of God
for their own contemporaries. But the theologians of liberation
maintain that they were forced to develop the theology of libera-

tion precisely in order to communicate with their contemporaries by taking account of the circumstances prevailing in Latin America. They insist that it is not a new theology, or a new theme emphasised within theology, but rather a new way of *doing* theology.

The contrast
As they see it, theologians in Europe and North America (north, for convenience) are preoccupied with articulating Christian faith to their contemporaries living in relative comfort, affluence and security and imbued with the 'enlightened, secularist, modern mentality'. Given this situation which conditions both themselves and their interlocutors, the theological preoccupation becomes 'How do we speak of God in a world come of age'? In stark contrast, Latin American (south) theologians are faced with a continent of poor, oppressed but believing people. They are victims of the 'structures of plunder' orchestrated on a worldwide scale but managed most immediately by powerful minorities within their own homelands. This situation of external dependency and internal domination inflicts suffering and misery on whole peoples and leaves whole classes systematically exploited and virtually enslaved, treated like beasts of burden, dehumanised. Their poverty is not a virtue; it is the hand of death laid on the living. Here the theologians' interlocutor is the 'non-person' and the theological preoccupation is: How can we speak of a God who is love, how can we say God is Father and that all are equally brothers and sisters, in a situation of massive in-human oppression (nearly always perpetrated by co-religionists)? How can we speak of salvation, of God's graciousness, in these inhuman, historical and political circumstances? How can we evangelise, proclaim 'good news' in action to people who have been actively victimised and consequently ravaged by hunger and sickness?

It was the pressure of these questions, arising out of the anguish of that context and acknowledged with a new urgency, that forced these southern theologians to radically rethink what it meant to be Christian and church. They felt called on to work out a new way of doing theology with its point of departure rooted in the Latin American reality, because the preoccupations and methodology of northern theology were not viable there. To 'do' theology there, according to the traditional models, would be to continue to offer theological legitimisation to a sinful situation. That situation would have to be tackled directly.

In speaking about the originality of their methodology they tend to represent northern theology as being overly theoretical and academic, reflecting the atmosphere of the universities and seminaries within which it is taught and written. Truth, they maintain, cannot be reached at a theoretical level in study by professors and then 'applied' pastorally by priests and pastoral agents. They are critical too of any privatisation of faith as if it did not need to be veri-fied, made true; or of any concern only with the doctrinal correctness of faith without stressing the need for its enfleshment.

These theologians wish to see theology emerging out of the correlation of common experience and Christian faith, as they struggle to articulate the consciousness of the Christian community living through the agony and hope of the present moment. But this correlation and articulation cannot be achieved in cool detachment in a study or library; it demands involvement and commitment. Its starting point is the actual life of the church, the commitment of Christians to transform the sinful reality of injustice within which they live.

Praxis
Here they introduce that much misunderstood word, praxis, with great frequency, to pinpoint the change in approach that is called for. Their meaning for the word is sometimes filtered through to the north, couched in unclarity. The emphasis on praxis and on the priority of praxis over theory, demanded by liberation theologians, is on occasion misrepresented by commentators as if they were advocating that people simply engage in some activity or other without real thought about the vision which should inform that activity. But praxis is not simply action or practice. It does not mean just 'putting the faith into practice'. Aristotle distinguished production and praxis. Skills and techniques may produce a house, but only virtuous parents and children can convert the house into a home. Praxis may be described in general terms as an activity engaged in, whose good is immanent within the activity itself.

Theologians of liberation use the word praxis to refer to a particular form of action that demands involvement and commitment, that enhances freedom, that struggles for transformation in society, that strives to be consistent with its own theory. It demands consistent involvement with the poor and the oppressed so as to develop personal and social freedom and liberation in society. It demands a new way of acting, a lifestyle and lifestructure that is an orthopraxis of love and justice.

Praxis, far from being blind, frenetic activity is always inspired by theory. There is always a 'dialect of theory and praxis' which is systematically suspicious of ideology. But to speak of the priority of praxis is to declare that praxis is the test and the norm and the critique of theory, and to offer a new criterion of truth. The New Testament warrant for this is found in texts like 'by their fruits you shall know them' and 'if anyone says I love God and hates his brother or sister, he is a liar'. Actual engagement in praxis, acting in solidarity with others, can correct and change the theory because it aims at transformative change in both the individual and society. It will thereby modify the theory as it changes the social reality out of which the theory emerged.

The conviction here is that people, despite the situation of oppression in which they live, can and must move beyond fatalism and enslavement and become subjects and shapers of their own destiny, models of more dedicated service, creators of a new world of greater liberty and freedom for all. Their hope derives from their faith in the gospel call to transform the social order and their conviction that the following of Jesus Christ must be made real in deed.

The movement
There is nothing mystifying about this, once we keep in mind the actual situation out of which liberation theology developed. Once someone becomes aware of the glaring inequalities of that situation, of the plight of 'the other' as anomalous, and begins to grasp something of the true causes of the injustice and death-bearing misery inflicted on the poor, they ask: What must we do as Christians in this situation? Why is there so much inhumanity in our so-called Christian country and continent? Christianity as they may have known it does not give a ready answer, for it may have been used by other Christians (and perhaps by themselves previously) to endorse the prevailing social order. Of necessity, they begin within a tradition but they now stand liminal to it and suspicious of any ideologising tendencies within it. So a

new appreciation of the correlation between the gospel and action for justice, a re-reading of the gospel in the light of the present situation and the present situation in the light of the gospel, is called for.

If this incipient 'conversion of the head', which may be accompanied by a sense of outrage at what is being done to fellow human beings, is to be nurtured, the theology of liberation insists that it must lead to a 'conversion of the feet', to a 'walking with the poor'. This movement from what I call sympathy with 'the anonymous poor' to solidarity with 'the poor who have a name' is indispensable. It means trying to see and experience the oppressive situation from the perspective of the poor, from what Metz calls 'the underside of history', from 'solidarity with the victims' (M Lamb). To really see things from the standpoint of the poor is not something that can be acquired through study or by doing a course, though many attempt it! It can only come from trying to experience life as they experience it, from involvement with and commitment to them, from making a 'preferential option for the poor'.

Option for the poor

This phrase has become somewhat of a cliché and has found its way into the documents of many northern religious congregations but, as always, actual praxis is the test of any set of words or theory. Liberation theologians point out that those involved in this process of conversion are called to opt for the poor, not because the poor are better or more holy, but because God is God and the poor are God's chosen ones. So direct experience of the poor and their poverty is only one more reason for the option. This prior commitment to the poor is insisted upon as the way to break the deterministic stranglehold of one's former worldview and self-protective rationalisations. Because of their former (unconscious) self-serving involvement in the structured injustices of society, and their consequent blindness to the plight of the oppressed, those now wishing to opt for the poor need to be brought face-to-face with the poor who bear in their very selves the consequences of those injustices. Hopefully they will be jolted into seeing that their own favoured status, their elitist privileges, were arrogated at the cost of the daily bread, indeed the very life blood, of the poor and the marginalised. Ongoing social analysis is needed to keep open the eyes that once were blind to the real structures of what sustained their former life-style and the minds that once found comfort in rationalisations of privilege.

From the moment they begin to 'cross over to the other side' (Mk 4:35) and begin to define the neighbour, not as the person next door nor as the one they meet along their way, but as the one whose way they now take, the one they 'go out to look for, on the highways and by-ways, in the factories and slums, on the farm and in the mines' (Gutierrez), their world is different. But this new praxis, although it is inspired by the Christian vision (*theoria*), brings them to pose new questions about Christianity: What does the faith mean? What does the bible say? How are we to evangelise in this situation where these people are being de-humanised? Who is God and what is God's relationship to this world? This re-reading of the bible and tradition goes on simultaneously with their practical commitment to the poor which makes it possible for them to hear the word of God in ever new ways. The theology of liberation has very ample biblical warrant for the priorities and emphases it proposes, although it is aware that its interpretation of scripture has at times been a little simplistic.

What the bible says
The bible is a record of the happening, the liberating event and the interpretative word between God and the poor. In history God is revealed as standing in judgement on human oppression and injustice, as taking the side of the poor, as being active to liberate his afflicted people. God's dream is to make justice reign, to remould a fragmented world 'nearer the heart's desire'. God is the 'father of orphans, defender of widows, who gives the lonely a permanent home and makes prisoners happy by setting them free'. (Ps 68:5-6) To know this God is not a matter of intellectual insight, rather knowledge (in the biblical sense) of God comes through doing justice (Jer 22:13-16), being involved in the liberation of others. Worship of God is an abomination without justice and love of the poor. (Is 1:10-17, 58:6-7) In the bible, to be just means loving what God loves. It means dealing with poor women and men as Yahweh dealt with the people when they were oppressed and enslaved. It means being able to hear the cry of the oppressed (Ex 3:7) and to respond to it actively. 'You must not pervert justice in dealing with a stranger or an orphan nor take a widow's garment in pledge. Remember that you were a

slave in Egypt and that Yahweh your God redeemed you from
there. That is why I lay this charge on you.' (Deut 24:17-18).

Exodus is the great paradigmatic event and is both a thoroughly
political act of liberation and a thoroughly salvific experience as
well . At its ultimate depth it is sustained by the God who liber-
ates. But that liberation is never complete and exile and servi-
tude and the expostulations of Job must never be forgotten;
hence the 'charge' laid on those who have come to experience at
least the beginnings of liberation. It is spelled out by all the
prophets (see Amos 2:6-7, Job 24:2-12). The charge is 'to bring
good news to the poor, to bind up hearts that are broken, to proclaim liberty to captives, freedom to those in prison and a jubilee
year of God's favour.' (Is 62:1-2) It means struggling to give the
future to those who by human reckoning have no future, struggling to bring about the kind of relationship between people
which Yahweh the God of justice desires, struggling to do for
oppressed people now, what Yahweh did for the enslaved people then. Within this biblical vision, to sin is to act unjustly. It is
to create relationships and structures and institutions founded
on unrightness, to become an oppressor, an enslaver. It means,
as Micah puts it, 'building Zion with blood and Jerusalem with
crime'.

Jesus the liberator

In the New Testament, 'the poor' refers to those who lack what
is necessary to make life human. It includes the 'bent over', the
'heavily burdened', the victims of 'man's inhumanity to man'.
Jesus enters into scandalising solidarity with them and treats
them as the privileged recipients of the good news of the kingdom of God. We must remember that Jesus did not simply
preach about God, but about the *kingdom* of God, that is, God
acting to transform the oppressive order of reality. And Jesus
enfleshed the presence and the power of the kingdom of God
through his own deeds. In his solidarity with the poor and the
outcasts, his table-fellowship with sinners, his healings and
exorcisms, the activity of God was taking concrete shape. On behalf of people who have no other hope of being liberated, Jesus
was active to offer integral humanisation. His preaching and
parables urged people to wake up from the dream of reality to
the reality of the dream of Yahweh, and to join together in service
of it. In opting for the poor, Jesus stood opposed to the people,

the structures, the institutes that 'bent people over'. He abhorred sin and evil and injustice and took up the struggle of the poor as his own so that it became his struggle for the poor and the oppressed. And because people understood only too well the radical character of his actions, the consequences of his struggle for justice, he was put to death . 'But God raised him from the dead.' In Jesus Christ the God of justice and freedom became history, pitched his tent in the midst of our pilgrim history. In him we say God became poor, he became the oppressed, became the victim, and constantly faced civil and religious oppressors with the truth about their oppression: It is against God that they have pitted themselves.

First and second acts

Liberation theology then starts from the life of the church and the poor, from pastoral action, from its commitment to evangelise. But it recognises that to be faithful to the gospel one must strive with the poor and the oppressed to build up a more just and more human society. This is Christian praxis and it is the first act. But as we saw, praxis gives rises to reflection even as one engages in it, for it provokes a re-reading of scripture and tradition in the light of this engagement which in turn calls for a deeper and more authentic commitment.

I have tried to indicate some of the biblical insights guiding this reflection. The rhythm of circularity is praxis-reflection-praxis. In the north, we dichotomise these inseparable moments and maintain that 'praxis is praxis and reflection is reflection' and so pose false problems for ourselves. By contrast, the theologians of liberation encourage reflection on praxis as one engages in it.

Gutierrez defines theology as 'critical reflection on Christian praxis in the light of the word of God.' He is adamant that theology is 'a second act', that it comes 'after' praxis (not chronologically but in terms of priority and relevance), that it arises out of a prior commitment to the poor. 'Active commitment to liberation comes first, theology develops from it.' Christian praxis is the response to the call of faith, and theology is reflection on that response. But this theology does not stop with reflection on the world but 'tries to be part of the process through which the world is transformed'. It does not exist for its own sake. Rather its goal is to make the commitment to the poor 'more self-critical and hence more comprehensive and radical'. The function of liberation theology is to reflect on and systematise what is actually happening, so that Christians may be able to insert themselves more deeply and effectively into that liberating praxis. It exists to further the struggle for life and against death in all forms.

With the poor

Being with the poor is not something passive. The struggle of the poor must become your struggle for the poor. And 'the poor' is a collective and conflictive noun. It is not a neutral concept. 'The poor' do not exist by choice or by nature or by fate, their existence has structural causes, their bondage is imposed by others. You voluntarily choose to be with the poor who are living in enforced poverty in order to proclaim that this poverty is contrary to the dream God has for people. So you must be with them in their struggle to live, become alert to the causes of injustice in that situation, help them to become aware of the social, political and economic structures of their society, and of their own fatalism within them, encourage them to become subjects. It means taking a real part in their struggle against all that oppresses them, and in their struggle for their human and civil rights – for clothing, health care, education, employment. 'Through the struggle against misery, injustice and exploitation the goal is the creation of a new man.' (Guiterrez) It will mean being a member with them in basic communities (or whatever local groupings there may be) – remembering that 'base' means the poor and the powerless – but only if you are really prepared to learn from them and let them lead you.

Being with the poor in their daily struggle does not mean that you can neglect the preaching of the gospel. Guiterrez strongly rejects any approach which says that you must first solve their social problems and then announce the gospel to them. To do so is to reinforce the attitude that the poor are non-persons, not yet on the same level as us. It is to be insensitive to the mysterious revelation of God among those who are God's special chosen ones, the poor. Ultimately he says it denies the first beatitude, 'Blessed are the poor'. Rather you must allow them to teach you what the gospel is since they are its privileged recipients and interpreters. With them you are called to denounce the injustices that are opposed to the kingdom and the gospel as good news to the poor. You must say who and what is responsible for these injustices and be a pressure source in conflictive situations.

Of the poor
If theology is to mean anything to the poor, it cannot be fabricated by others and offered to them. It must be a theology of the vanquished and the victims if it is not to continue the cycle of oppression. Evangelisation, the theologians of liberation claim, will only be genuinely liberating when the poor themselves become its messengers. Then the preaching of the gospel will indeed become a stumbling block! But the gospel proclaimed in this new way will call together a church of the people, a church gathered from among the poor and the marginalised and through them gathering together all humankind, like the parable of the great feast.

These themes of being evangelised by the poor, of discipleship of the poor, of letting their voice be heard without mediation, have been present in liberation theology from the beginning, but often they were more a sincere wish than a reality until the late seventies. They have since become the dominant concern for many theologians of liberation and this marks a significant second stage of development. Given the nature and setting of its genesis, and the complexity and subtlety of its approach (e.g. use of social analysis), it is understandable that its primary field of force was among students and middle class people struggling to respond to the gospel in a world of poverty and oppression. Here it was extraordinarily successful and many people turned from their role as conscious or unconscious oppressors to struggle for the liberation of the poor.

But this option, however costly and admirable, was *for* the poor. Their strivings, their denunciations were for and on behalf of the marginalised. And while it did bring about substantial betterment of the lot of many poor people, the majority of them were unable to understand its total 'language' and so become its active agents. Those without a voice were still being spoken for through intermediaries. So while southern theologians were criticising their northern colleagues for being too intellectual and academic, the poor were often voicing the same complaint about those struggling for them at the local level. But there the complaint was heard and responded to effectively.

In this second phase, at a new level of conversion, the teachers are becoming the taught, the speakers are becoming the listeners, the theologians are liberating themselves from their former roles and are learning how oppressed people live their faith. Particular interest is being shown in the 'popular religiosity' of the poor, which tended to be bypassed in earlier years in order to present them with more 'liberative' forms. This concentration of energy on 'crossing over', on 'becoming one with the other', has meant that the theologians are thinking and writing in a different way and are no longer looking northwards for approval as they write. They are concerned to reflect the values inherent in the 'culture of the oppressed', to communicate their own experience of poor persons as the privileged revealers of the crucified God and the Christ.

Spirituality
That last point raises the question of spirituality which, from the beginning, has had a central place in the theology of liberation. Gutierrez points out that the differences between the various approaches in theology (Dominican, Franciscan, etc) is located in their spirituality, for spirituality is the matrix of all theology. So the methodology adopted by liberation theology tells us what its spirituality is, for it aims, through concrete actions, to call Christians to evangelical conversion, which is the heart of all spirituality. This is conversion to the God who first loved us, a realignment of self to that God's priorities. That God is to be loved through loving the neighbour. They are to deepen their faith, their love, their compassion in response to those in need. Love of neighbour cannot ignore the social structures that oppress and diminish his/her life so they are called to be contemplatives in political action, linking love with the demands of social justice. 'For many Christian Latin American leaders ... a theology of liberation would be, at its best, spiritual theology ... a study of the inspirational themes and evangelical motivations that lie behind any Christian action for the sake of justice and the liberation of the poor.' (Galilea) But instead of speaking of a 'spirituality of liberation', it would be more accurate to talk about a spirituality 'in times of liberation' or 'in cultures or societies in need of liberation'. At any rate, it would be 'a synthesis of evangelical values and personal motivation, inspiring different forms of solidarity with the poor, and nourished in turn by the experience of solidarity and compassion'. (Galilea) It is the spirituality of the Magnificat.

Theology

Southern theologians are adamant that the primacy of praxis is what is missing from northern theology and that its absence has very serious consequences. Metz's charge in the 1960s that the categories most prominent in theology were 'the intimate, the private, the apolitical', they feel, has not been completely refuted. The theology of liberation rejects the idealism that it sees as characteristic of much northern theology – that one can reach truth in a theoretical way, which can then be applied practically in more or less imperfect ways. In fairness it must be said that this is an overstatement, but their basic intuition remains true, that northern theologians have not understood truth as transformation, as what is perceived in the struggle for justice, for human rights (and against oppression) in society. It is on the question, What is truth?, that the real battles between theologians north and south have been and will be fought.

Both sides agree that love is the heart of Christianity and that we truly love God by loving the neighbour. When southern theologians declare that love must be linked to the demands of justice, that salvation is not just a goal at the end of history but a process happening in history, that it includes social, economic and political release from oppressive structures, many in the north will agree. But when they go on to spell out what this means concretely, especially in terms of the theologians' own involvement, they begin to draw fire and even the most sympathetic tend to say 'this prior commitment to the poor is all right in South America, things are different there' or 'a splendid idea for non-theologians, but the real research must go on, you know'.

The gnostic tendency

Here they touch a raw nerve (or lack of nerve) and pinpoint what I would call the gnostic tendency present in the northern approach to theology, which does not see an intrinsic connection between practical commitment and the task of theology. Northern theologians and biblical scholars appeal to the need for 'detachment', for 'scholarship and reflection', and take refuge in their 'critical function'. Southern theologians do not at any time deny the need for this, but they ask about the missing link between study and the transformation of society, 'Theology … is more interested in being liberative than in talking about liberation'. (Segundo) 'What price is paid for this detachment and objectivity?' they ask. In fact they say that this detachment and this neutrality are not what they appear to be but actually connive with the injustices of our society. Political innocence or even neutrality is not possible. Northern theology does not recognise that its apparent 'objectivity' in fact always emerges out of a particular political stance – that which is in favour of the status quo. The supports for their study and research and lifestyle come from consumerism and capitalism, and are ultimately bought at the expense of the poor.

Two thirds of the population of our one world, planet Earth, are hungry. On an average day forty thousand children are killed by malnutrition and related disease. In an average year at least twenty-nine million people starve to death and the toll is rising. UNICEF experts say the number of children dying from hunger will increase by one third by 2000 AD. For every child that dies of malnutrition, six more live on, their lives permanently scarred by hunger and ill health. They do not have the energy to grow and to learn. This horrific scenario is not the product of fate or nature, for much of it is due to human causes, to social and political factors, which could be changed.

Liberation theology suggests that the theological problem is not 'man come of age' but rather all those who are victims and who 'die before their time'. The problem now facing all theology and all theologians is the problem of the non-person. How can we continue to talk of a provident creator God or salvation in Christ or the meaning of human life, in such a world of massive suffering and injustice and oppression of God's people? Theology, they insist, must respond to the scandal of this oppression and death, for it reveals the universal dimensions of human sin and calls into question the very meaning of human life and the reality of God. Theology has other issues to attend to, but if it does not focus on this crisis of our time, which threatens the entire Christian message, it is declaring its own irrelevance and impotence. If theologians do not challenge this crisis, they condone it and do so as representatives of Christian faith. The theology of liberation maintains that theologians cannot stand apart from this crisis. But it is not enough to reflect on it; they themselves must be engaged in the work for justice and freedom if what they say about salvation is to be credible. They cannot sit on the fence composing 'foreign policy' for others to implement. They must make concrete historical choices. Of course, for southern theologians the actuality of salvation becomes apparent in praxis. A prior commitment to the poor and the oppressed is called for. And it is here that many northern theologians refuse to follow them.

The challenge accepted

But their challenge remains and some northern theologians are trying to respond to it. The response in fact involves conversion of the head and feet and heart. These theologians have begun to recognise that they themselves are part of the problem. They do not wish any longer to condone the unjust world order by refusing critically to protest against it. They do not wish to live any longer insulated from the experience of the poor, for they are convinced that this provides the key. They have grown tired of the internecine wrangling among scholars. They no longer believe in their once fond hope that logic and rhetoric and the appeal to the 'nobler self', or even personal conversion, would lead to a change in unjust structures. They believe now that if they want social justice they must work for change in a discerning way. They must make a choice, be prepared to dirty their shoes and their hands, and turn their backs on the gnostic wisdom of 'whatever you say, do nothing'! They believe that there is something great in honest failure.

Of course they agree that we need reflection and a vision of the new world that is to be created, but how much reflection and theory do people need before they begin to act? Why should the movement be always one-way – from theory to practice, from right thinking to right living, from orthodoxy to orthopraxis? Why do people presume that theory and insight will somehow change the world where injustice has congealed into 'institutionalised violence'? Why isn't more time given to search actively for the 'missing link' of how to translate theory into liberative action? There is more involved in bringing about social transformation, structural reform and real equality, than changing your own mind, surely.

By doing the truth one comes to know truth. What one does, how one acts, makes one's profession of faith credible or incredible. To engage in the prophetic ministry of theologian is to be in quest of an alternative vision (God's dream). But if it does not also involve one in the actual struggle to enflesh that vision, one is open to the charge levelled against 'those who sit on the chair of Moses'. 'Anyone who ventures to speak to people of justice must first be just in their own eyes.' (*Justice in the World*)

In the north, we may have successfully banished the poor from our thoughts and our tables, but we are always present at their table as those who have devoured their share. When we realise that, have we the gall to continue sitting there theorising?

Grace, salvation and sacrament
Human hopes for completion and fulfilment in freedom and transcendence, have always been conditioned by the painful experience of the absence of such fulfilment. Israel's hopes for salvation and her longing for wholeness were projected out of situations characterised by suffering and oppression. The theology of liberation too, as we have seen, sprang from the painful tension between dis-graceful poverty and oppression on a massive scale and the Christian conviction about God's gracious salvation. From its inception, it has wrestled with the question of how the existence of evil on such an incalculable scale can be reconciled with faith in a gracious God. These theologians know that the only credible proclamation of salvation is one which takes account of human sinfulness and the history of human suffering and shows how they can be creatively related, at least in principle and certainly in practice, to one's convictions about salvation.

Their writings have shocked us into a new awareness of the blood, sweat and tears that constitutes the history of suffering for Latin American people. But they have also alerted us to the socio-political dimensions of human sinfulness and our own complicity in so much evil, even where formal guilt may not be assigned. They acknowledge, as other theologians do, the personal and interpersonal implications and consequences of sin, but they have also emphasised the communal, institutional and systemic reality of sin and have forced (or freed) other theologians to explore these dimensions.

Behind these new insights into the reality of sin, lies the conviction that is verified above all to their approach to grace and salvation, namely that individual, personalist categories do not measure up to the fullness of human being. Beyond these categories, actual historical human existence must be understood as interdependent and co-responsible, as socialised in relation to the life-patterns, structures and institutions of a specific culture and society, as involved in the social construction of reality, as ecologically related. Following the teaching of Rahner and Vatican II on the universal availability of grace, they see grace and salvation operative as a liberating force in all these dimensions of human life. Consequently our response to that grace cannot be confined to the personal and interpersonal spheres but must be embodied in transformative concern for all these dimensions of human existence. They are critical of interpretations of salvation that emphasised its relation only to the 'soul' or to life after death or that did not adequately represent the 'social and political arenas as *loci* for encounter with God's gracious saving presence. They recall that Yahweh not only forgave Israel's sins but sought her social and political liberation as well and that Jesus was concerned with both sin and the consequences of sin, but above all with 'life to the full' (Jn 10:10). Salvation must be personal and political, universal and particular. Related to this is their insight into the unity of the human race, their frequent invocation of the watch-word 'solidarity', their appeal to the 'people' – all of which sound strange to northern ears but resonate perfectly with biblical anthropology. Following Rahner, they understand grace as God's self-communication to human beings but move beyond his near identification of grace and spirit to fully identity.

Salvation is then seen as the power of God's spirit working within the human spirit, liberating it from sin and bondage and freeing it for commitment to love. The text, 'For freedom Christ has set us free' (Gal 5:1) is taken as a summary of their approach and they insist that, in the scripture and in Christian testimony, God's Spirit working in human existence takes the form of liberation, of freed freedom. They see the Spirit at work in the process of freeing from sin that distorts and poisons human freedom, in empowering humanisation, in opening up shared concern for common humanity and in overcoming dehumanising structures. Salvation is presented as liberation by the Spirit of God. This is what grounds their positive convictions about history as the locus where God's grace/Spirit is encountered and about praxis as giving meaning to history.

The question of the dialectical relationship of salvation and liberation has been the subject of much debate. The scriptural, anthropological and magisterial warrants for using the master-image of liberation, are unquestionable and the power of its appeal is indisputable. But once again we must remember that no single model – even if we judge it to be the best – can adequately communicate the mystery of the divine-human relationship. The stress given to the kingdom symbol and to eschatology by theologians of liberation provides safeguards against any simplistic identification of salvation and social, political and economic emancipation. Yet they rightly stress that where love, peace, and justice are found, they are the fruits of the Spirit and so first-fruits of final and definitive salvation.

A more difficult question is the understanding of the ambivalence of human freedom in some of their writings. While they are justly critical of institutional and systemic oppression, they may sometimes appear to be naïvely optimistic about how power will be exercised within the structures and systems with which they propose to replace them. Freeing freedom may indeed overcome some of the oppressive structures which derive from the sinful abuse of human freedom, but it will not necessarily eradicate sin itself, which is the source of these pathological expressions. The oppressors, the oppressed and the newly liberated are all prone to the corruption of freedom. Only radical ongoing conversion through the Spirit's grace, which renews the relationship between God, the self and others, can bring about a situation that does not give rise to further oppression.

Finally, these theologians see worship as playing a vital role in the process of liberation. They are opposed to any quasi-magical understanding of sacraments and insist on the consistent intrinsic relationship between the integrity of the liberating struggles of daily life and the authenticity of liturgy. 'If you are offering your gift at the altar, and there remember that your brother or sister has something against you, leave your gift there before the altar and go, first be reconciled to your brother or sister, and then come and offer your gift' (Mt 5:23-24), is taken as a guideline text to their whole approach. In line with this emphasis, they maintain that the historical Jesus of Nazareth is the primary referent for understanding the sacraments and liturgy. It is in his life and ministry that we see liberation and salvation taking place. In the liturgy, through the power of the Spirit of the risen

Christ, we are challenged once again by his prophetic word. There too, through the mediation of the church's symbols, we re-appropriate the salvation of Jesus Christ and are challenged to live lives of love and service in his memory.

'Let every word be the fruit of action and reflection. Reflection alone without action, or tending towards it, is merely theory, adding its weight when we are overloaded with it already; and it has led the young to despair. Action alone without reflection is being busy pointlessly. Honour the Word eternal and speak to make a new world possible.' (Helder Camara)

Note

1. This chapter first appeared in *The Mount Oliver Review*, 1986. It was intended as an introduction to the theology of liberation and was based mainly on the writings of Gustavo Gutierrez. A new ending has been added here.

CHAPTER 8

Theology and symbolic ritual

'A wonder told shyly'
(Austin Clarke)

This chapter begins by recalling the scholastic theology that existed before the Council and the developments that have taken place since. It then seeks to explore the nature of ritual, symbol and narrative, and their relevance to life and liturgy.

Scholastic theology of sacrament
The Council of Trent taught that 'if anyone says that the sacraments of the new law do not contain the grace they signify, or that they do not confer the same grace on him or her who places no obstacle to it ... or that grace is not conferred *ex opere operato* through the sacraments of the new law, but that faith alone in the divine promises is sufficient to obtain grace: let him or her be anathema.' (D. 1606,1608) These canons were formulated in reaction to the positions of the Reformers and enunciated the minimum necessary for maintaining Catholic doctrine. After Trent, however, these statements became the main planks of the scholastic teaching on the sacraments.

Their overall approach tended to treat the sacraments as 'objective' realities instituted by Christ whose nature and purpose could be clarified by posing certain questions. What exactly is it that is done to us by our using a sacrament? Who can administer a sacrament and how much depends on the person of the minister? To what extent do my personal dispositions enter into the process?

In itself, *ex opere operato* (Literally, 'by the work done', i.e. effective by means of the rite itself.) could mean what it had meant in the earlier writings of Thomas Aquinas (it is not found in the *Summa*), 'through the redemptive mystery of Christ alone'. This demanded that the minister act according to the mind of the church. Similarly, the phrase to 'place no obstacle', used by Trent to apply to both adults and children, had previously been understood as implying that personal faith, love and surrender entered into the very essence of sacraments and not merely as demanding freedom from sin. Both *ex opere operato* and *ex opere operantis* (which takes account of the dispositions of the recipient) were necessary for a true sacrament yet, in scholastic teaching, these phrases were used to contrast the bestowal of grace with the subjective dispositions of the recipient. In the manuals, in the classroom and from the pulpit, they were heard as justifying an automatic, minimalistic view of the sacraments. Accordingly people formed an image of the church as an institution for 'dispensing' or administering sacraments. These were seen as means of grace administered by a priest for the salvation of the rather passive recipients who placed no obstacle to their efficacy. The concerns of that theology with the minimum requirements for validity, with matter and form, with debates about causality and instrumentality, when combined with the rather physical categories it used for speaking about grace, did conspire to give the impression that the sacramental realm was characterised by the impersonal, the calculable and the minimal.

Scholastic theology did relate the sacraments very strongly to Christ, but unfortunately it was to a Christ whose divinity was emphasised at the expense of his humanity. Furthermore, Christ was considered in isolation from Father and Spirit. And the point of concentration was Christ's passion and death (his life and resurrection were not considered to be important). The link between priest and sacrament was strong, but the relationship between church and sacrament was tenuous. When this approach to sacraments was combined with the nature/supernature understanding of grace and salvation, it was very difficult to see sacraments as celebrations, as worship, as involving community.

The translation

Those of us who attended primary and post-primary school before the Second Vatican Council, were given a sawn-off version of that theology and were taught to look on sacraments as holy things which were means of getting grace, or 'as channels of grace'. We were taught to be very concerned with what we got out of sacraments rather than what we put into them. But we were told about the importance of dispositions, about how we

could merit other graces if we were rightly disposed, and images contrasting thimbles and buckets were used. We learned to
distinguish between sacraments of the living and sacraments of
the dead (baptism and penance). We worried, for example,
about what would happen someone who received confirmation
without being in the state of grace, since it could only be received once – would it revive when they made a good confes-
sion? We were taught to see life in the world as unholy and
fraught with temptation. We were encouraged to strive to be
'good' but in practice it seemed like a difficult game of spiritual
snakes and ladders. In the daily struggle with 'the world, the
flesh and the devil' it was assumed that we would sin frequently.
Or, if we managed to stay in the state of grace, we would experience ourselves as weakened and vulnerable and in need of
sacramental grace to recharge the spiritual batteries. So if we
needed penance as a sacrament of the dead, or communion as
sacrament of the barely-living, we would withdraw from the
sinful world to a holy place at a holy time where, through the
mediation of a holy thing administered by a holy person, we
would either return to the state of grace or receive an increase of
grace. Mass was the Sunday obligation (communion was for
those who managed to remain in the state of grace) and we
knew it to be 'the same sacrifice as that of Calvary though offered in an unbloody manner'. At Mass we were to rid ourselves
of all distractions, close our eyes to those around us and pray
privately (though I remember vividly the drone of the public
recitation of the rosary at Mass during May and October).
Someone else was doing something out there for us and we
were told how best to take part in preparation for the great miracle of the consecration when the priest brought Christ down on
the altar.

'Heaven dazzled death.
Wonder should I cross-plough that turnip-ground?
The tension broke. The congregation lifted its head
as one man and coughed in unison.'
(P. Kavanagh, *The Great Hunger*, 4)

Changes
Meanwhile, all unbeknowst to us, things were changing. The
encyclicals of Pius XII in the 1940s encouraged a renewed appreciation of the scriptures, of the church as the body of Christ, of the

liturgy. Encouraged by these developments, those involved in the liturgical movement took their conference to Assisi in 1956 and, within a couple of years, John XXIII announced that he was calling the Vatican Council.

Soon we were asked to move away from the old ingrained ways of worship. We were called from passivity to participation, from an emphasis on the individual to community, from what we got out of sacraments to giving ourselves into the mystery, from seeing sacraments as holy things to seeing them as liturgical actions, from praying at Mass to praying the Mass. It must be said that the sacramental theology of the scholastics was seriously at variance with the theology which was explicit and implicit in the *Constitution on the Sacred Liturgy*. Yet the vast majority of those charged with the implementation of liturgical reform were trained in the ways of scholastic theology. When we become aware of this deep irony, we may wonder how the renewal was even as successful as it was.

Rahner and Schillebeeckx
Was any kind of alternative sacramental theology available to accompany the renewal of the liturgical life of the church? By an interesting coincidence, 1963 saw not only the promulgation of the *Constitution on the Sacred Liturgy* but also the publication in English of two significant books on sacramental theology: *Christ the Sacrament* (a summary of a work published in 1952) by Edward Schillebeeckx[1] (S) and *The Church and the Sacraments* by Karl Rahner[2] (R). Both of them sought to redress the imbalances of the scholastic approach by proposing that a deeper understanding of both church and sacrament would be mutually enriching. Scholastic theology had confined the concept of sacrament exclusively to the seven rites of the church. However a more ancient tradition had used *mysterium* and *sacramentum* as synonymous and interchangeable terms. Out of that rich, biblical and patristic tradition it made sense for them to speak of 'Christ the sacrament of God' and the church as 'the primordial sacrament'. Their approach set out to be profoundly christological and ecclesiological. They broke through the isolation in which the sacraments had been kept and managed to weave together theologies of God, revelation, Christ, church, sacraments and Christian life. These they combined in very powerful and fruitful ways with insights from anthropology and phenomenology.

Basically they affirmed that God's approach to human beings has always been essentially sacramental. Grace wherever it is found 'never comes just interiorly; it confronts us in visible shape as well'. (S.9) This tendency towards visibility reached its climax in the flesh of Jesus of Nazareth, 'the word of God, God's last word uttered into the visible public history of mankind, a word of grace, reconciliation and eternal life: Jesus Christ.' (R.15) The power and graciousness of God reached men and women of his time through the preformative words and declaratory actions of Jesus of Nazareth; they took visible form, were sacramental. All these gracious contacts, all these bestowals of salvation and grace between Jesus and his contemporaries, took place in and through human meetings or personal *encounters* (mediated, as is every human exchange, through bodily presence.) 'The man Jesus is the personal, visible realisation of the divine grace of redemption, is the sacrament, the primordial sacrament because this man, the son of God himself is intended by the Father to be in his humanity the only way to the actuality of redemption. (S.16) Or as Rahner puts it: 'Christ is the historically real and actual presence of the eschatologically victorious mercy of God ... through whom the whole of mankind is in principle already accepted for salvation ... the fate of the world has been finally decided.' (R.14-15)

His deeds and words also expressed his own total dependence on the Father for they are acts of wondering praise and heartfelt thanksgiving. He is the supreme worshipper of the Father expressing in himself the perfect human response to the graciousness of God. In the Passover of his death, he hands himself over to the Father in self-sacrificing love and 'receives the glory that the father would give him'. (S.31) Schilleebeckx insists that we must not see the incarnation, life, ministry, death, resurrection and sending of the Spirit as discrete events, but as unified moments in a single process. Consequently everything expressed and achieved in his life and death remained eternally-enduring in the risen Christ who has become the sender of the Spirit.

But does the visibility principle and the incarnational structure of communication between God and human beings come to an end with the death of Jesus Christ? Schilleebeckx and Rahner maintain that God remains true to the principles of the incarnation and still offers God's self as grace in visible form through the church, in the liturgy. 'Christ makes his presence among us actively visible and tangible too, not directly through his own bodiliness, but by extending among us on earth in visible form the function of his bodily reality which is in heaven. This is precisely what the sacraments are: the earthly extension of the 'body of the Lord'. This is the church. (S.49)

But the church should not be seen as somehow simply prolonging the historical life of Jesus, rather it 'bridges the gap' between Christ in glory and the as-yet unglorified members of his Body. For Rahner, the church 'is the continuance, the contemporary presence, of that real, eschatologically triumphant and irrevocably established presence in the world, in Christ, of God's salvific will. The church is the abiding presence of that primal sacramental word of definitive grace, which Christ is in the world, effecting what is uttered by uttering it in sign. By the very fact of being in that way the enduring presence of Christ in the world, the church is truly the fundamental sacrament, the well-spring of the sacraments in the strict sense. From Christ, the church has an intrinsically sacramental structure.' (R.18) Schillebeeckx emphasises the unique once-for-all character of Christ's redemption, and sees the sacraments 'as ecclesial acts of worship in which the church in communion with its heavenly head … pleads with the Father for the bestowal of grace on the recipient of the sacrament and in which at the same time the church itself, as saving community in holy union with Christ, performs a saving act'.(S.79) In their sacramental trajectory, the man Jesus is the sacrament of God, the church is the sacrament of Christ and God, and the ritual actions of the church are sacraments of the presence and action of Christ and God.

Their approach to sacraments goes back behind the scholastic tradition and recovers the biblical, patristic and Thomistic foundations of sacramental theology. It is not only profoundly christological and ecclesiological, but it also manages to offer a powerful synthesis of the theologies of God, revelation, faith and Christian life. In line with the personalist/encounter model above, they moved away from seeing sacraments as 'sacred things' and presenting grace as quantifiable. Instead they use language that is relational and personal, and the category of 'being present' replaces the category of 'being there'. The validity of their foundational insights received confirmation in the documents of Vatican II.

There we find that the need to maintain the centrality of Christ and the church in whatever may be said about the sacraments is stressed; a broad understanding of sacrament is seen to be applicable to the church itself; there is a movement away from seeing sacraments as 'sacred things' towards appreciating them as worshipful actions of the whole church; they are understood to give faith-full expression to the church's identity and mission.

These works of Schillebeeckx and Rahner had a lasting influence on students of theology in the 1960s and into the 70s, although as is obvious from the few quotations above, neither work made for easy reading. Further writings from both men continued to influence sacramental theology both directly and indirectly.

A Copernican revolution
In 1970, Rahner published an article which was translated into English as 'How to receive a sacrament and mean it'.[3] In it he proposed a 'Copernican revolution in Catholic thinking about sacraments: instead of seeing in them a spiritual movement outward from the sacramental system to an effect in the world, we should look for a spiritual movement of the world toward the sacrament.' He believed that the new approach could more easily address the difficulties that even dedicated Catholics had in experiencing the Mass as the 'summit and source of the Christian life'. (S.C.) Those difficulties derived partly from the tension between the rhetoric of desiring to live authentically and the profound level at which that free disposition of themselves had to be enacted; partly from the fane/profane dichotomy in their interpretation of life, which tended to see the sacraments as isolated, discrete discharges of grace into an otherwise profane world. By contrast, in his vision, 'the world is permeated by God's grace ... permanently graced at its root, the inmost centre of the conscious subjects'. God's self-communication of grace is at the heart of everything and everyone and it attained its clearest, paradigmatic manifestation in Jesus of Nazareth who was God's irreversible, gracious, last word. This grace, as the deepest meaning and the ultimate depth of all that is, creates a powerful solidarity among people as is visibly exemplified in the church.

The church should not be seen as a sign of salvation only for those who belong to it; rather it is the basic sacrament of God's grace and salvation for the whole world. It is 'the visible community of those who confess that God offers everyone salvation

through the death and resurrection of his Christ' and who r
that sacramentally manifest in their solidarity with others.
sacraments are acts of that church when it freely commits itself
at decisive moments in the life of the community and the individual, and as such signify the grace that the church signifies.
Sacraments must be seen as springing from, expressing and
leading to the divine depths of real life.

This is how he applies all of this to the eucharist: 'The world and
its history is a terrifying, sublime, death-and-immolation liturgy
which God celebrates unto himself by the agency of mankind
…'. But we ignore this liturgy of the world so it must be 'clarified and brought to reflex awareness in what we ordinarily call
liturgy'. According to this vision, 'going to Mass, then, adds
nothing to the world but celebrates what is really happening in
the world. Jesus' cross is not raised again, but its mysterious
presence in the world is put into words. At Mass, the Christian
offers the world in bread and wine, knowing that the world is
already offering itself in triumph and tears and blood to the
incomprehensible, which is God. He gazes into ineffable light,
knowing that the real vision is given to eyes blinded with tears
or glassy with approaching death. He knows that he proclaims
the death of the Lord because this death is ever present in the
heart of the world and in everyone who "dies in the Lord." He
proclaims the Lord's coming, because he is coming in whatever
brings the world closer to its goal. He receives the true body of
the Lord, knowing it would profit him nothing, were he not in
communion with the body of God which is the world itself with
its fate. He hears and speaks the word of God, aware that it is the
verbal expression of the divine word which is the world, and of
the Word in which God eternally says 'yes' to this world.'

Further developments
In the late 1960s and during the 1970s, other authors built on the
achievements of Rahner and Schillebeeckx but added their own
unique contributions to sacramental theology. In retrospect it is
possible to link their works to one or other of the models mentioned in the previous chapter, and to notice the influence of
personalist philosophy or developmental psychology or process
philosophy or the social sciences on their work. In the 1970s as
well, a number of writers attempted to renew the understanding
of the sign-character of sacraments and sacramental causality

through an exploration of the nature and function of symbol. The sources here were social anthropologists, historians of religious forms, philosophers, psychologists and theologians (Rahner, *The Theology of the Symbol*, T.I. vol. 4 was very important). At the same time, studies which sought to apply psychological and anthropological insight into the nature of ritual to the rites of the church began to appear. (It is another of the ironies of that period that the Roman Catholic Church undertook to renew its ritual forms without studying the nature of ritual.) Similar concerns continued to characterise publications in the 1980s, but a change of focus began to be discernible. Previously, occasional books and articles had tried to take the texts and the actual liturgical celebration of individual sacraments as the basis for theological investigation. This began to be accepted as the norm and the emphasis began to be laid much more on liturgical theology rather than on sacramental theology. The total experience of the liturgical celebration itself, and not merely the text of the rites, was now seen as a theological *locus*, (some would say *the* theological *locus*).

Liturgical theology
Liturgical theology (or more accurately theologies) is still evolving the appropriate methodology to be used by it is a controverted question and there is no definition of it which enjoys universal support. However this much is clear, it proposes a comprehensive approach which combines evaluation of the assembly's actual experience of and response to liturgy, with an exploration of the symbols, language, gestures and history of the ritual action with reflection on the texts of the tradition. (These chapters are, I hope, a modest attempt to take that approach seriously.) Perhaps we could risk a generalisation and say quite simply that theologians have come to recognise that the liturgy is praxis. In keeping with the understanding of praxis outlined in the previous chapter, such a recognition demands that we give priority to the actual celebration of liturgy which is to be appreciated as a good in itself (not done for something outside the eucharistic celebration). It also requires us to see liturgical theology as part of the necessary dialectic of reflection and praxis, an ongoing exploration of the interface between life and liturgy, between what we proclaim and enact. Finally it asks that we pay attention to the worshipping subjects in the liturgy. This is a further encour-

agement to and empowerment of participants to become active subjects rather than passive onlookers in the ritual process.

A gracious approach

These new developments promise to have a profound impact on both the theology of sacramental rituals and their actual celebration but they will also have repercussions on all areas of theology. We might represent it in this way: In the famous analogy of Lao Tzu, mystery is said to be like the hole of the centre of a wheel. It is only because of the hole at the centre that the wheel exists and functions at all. It appears to be nothing, a mere void yet its influence is all-pervasive for it sustains not only the spokes and the felloes but the in-between spaces as well. The spokes converge on it but must never enter it, they must 'know their place' and ensure that it must never be filled in. Unfortunately, spokes within the theological wheel have not always known their place but have claimed to know too much, to have access to the Centre, to have authority granted by it to speak on its behalf. We have seen how theologies of grace and salvation, which should have been marked by particular sensitivity to the gracious mystery, failed in especially painful ways to maintain respectful distance and proceeded to divide and dissect and define. It seems that recent developments in liturgical theology are seeking to rectify such distortions and to ensure that our discourse about and celebration of, the mystery of God's graciousness, will be deeply respectful and doxological. Such theology would not exist to solve problems but to prevent us from dissolving mystery. By contrast with a theology that claimed to know too much, and with celebrations that tended to be didactic in a heavy-handed way, the guideline for this newer approach would be one of 'wonder told shyly'. Such reverential diffidence in the presence of wonder, such a desire to incorporate feelings, values and meaning, could help us realise that our celebrations are always about the 'hint half-guessed, the gift half-understood' (Eliot), so that they should be evocative, suggestive and above all imaginative. And by insisting that all approaches to the mystery 'know their place', liturgical theology should breakdown the compartmentalisation still found in religious studies, and build bridges between the many areas of human study that should be allowed to enrich our appreciation of liturgy. To serve as a focus for such an enterprise, liturgical theology itself would have to be 'roomy and broad' (to recall the biblical image for salvation) and always incomplete.

Since its subject is God's gracious liberation, it should itself be gracious and liberating.

Ritual origins

The concentration on the ritual event that characterises this new movement within liturgical theology has reinforced the need for ongoing exploration of narrative, ritual and symbol. We must attend to these subjects for the remainder of this chapter.

Taking our cue from liturgical theology itself, ideally our approach should start from an actual celebration and pay serious attention to the relevant texts. Such an undertaking however is quite simply beyond the scope of this chapter. As a compromise we will try to work with a very familiar ritual occasion when the eucharist speaks most powerfully about itself. It tells its best stories and invites us to engage in its most dramatic rituals at the evening Mass of the Lord's Supper on Holy Thursday.

The liturgy of the word of that Mass makes it very clear that, if we want to understand the eucharist, we must look first to the life, death and new life of Jesus of Nazareth and, secondly, to the life and worship of Israel. The gospel tells us that when the time had come for Jesus to pass over from this world to the Father, when he was face to face with death, he engaged in ritual. During the supper he washed his disciples' feet. He 'the Lord and master' performs an action that was then regarded as so menial that it should be done only by a slave or so intimate that it could be done only by a wife for her husband. It is an extraordinary act of both service and intimacy that sums up his entire life and ministry. Afterwards he tells them: 'I have given you an example that you may copy what I have done.' It is to become a distinguishing ritual for disciples who 'should wash each other's feet'. These commands are parallel to the commands that we find in the second reading, referring to the ritual of bread and wine. There Paul recounts what 'the Lord Jesus' said and did at table with his disciples on the 'night that he was betrayed'. Paul then tells us that 'until the Lord comes, everytime you eat this bread and drink this cup, you are proclaiming his death'. These ritual actions are of eschatological significance and will continue until the end of time.

The liturgy of the word is not content to offer us these two rituals, it adds a third from the Book of Exodus. It tells of the command given to the Jewish people of God to prepare and eat a

meal together that ritualises their story of enslavement and liberation. Equivalently it is saying that, if we do not appreciate
what covenant, sacrifice, memorial, blessing, eating a meal together meant for these people, we will not understand what a
Jew called Jesus, in the company of Jewish disciples, was doing
on that night.

Scripture scholars tell us that they can detect in the Passover text
from Exodus a conflation of two earlier feasts. One involved the
ritual killing and eating of a spring lamb, the other a ritual associated with eating the first, unleavened bread of the harvest.
Presumably rituals involving first fruits from the crops and the
flocks were part of the repertoire of the 'fathers who served
other Gods beyond the river and in Egypt' (Jos 24:14), before
they were brought into line with the worship of Yahweh.
Genesis brings us further back to the dawn of history by linking
these rituals to those of Cain, who 'brought the Lord an offering
of the fruit of the ground, and Abel brought of the firstlings of
his flock ...' (Gen 4:3-4) Rituals associated with the flocks among
nomadic people, and with crops among agrarian people, played
a very important role in the rise of the great world religions.
And beyond that development no doubt, 'our dark fathers and
mothers' (B. Kennelly) used configurations of earth and water,
fire and air, to ritualise their relationship to some transcendent
force. There may even be a basis for asserting that 'man was a
ritualist before he could speak'[4] or for suspecting that every significant ritual we have as human beings was engendered by
some crucial breakthrough in the development of the human
race. Of course archaeology or palaeontology may never yield
the evidence needed to support such a hypothesis, but there is
surely something archetypal in the human response to fire –
whether of the hearth, or the bonfire or the tamed fire that is a
candle. Or think of the elaborate rituals which surround cooking
food rather than eating it raw, which rest back on the breakthrough for humanity represented in its discovery and control
of fire which enabled it to survive the ice-ages. (On a different
level, the linguistic roots of the word 'ritual' are very ancient
and derive from the proto-Indo-European morpheme *rt*.)

Even if the genesis point of significant rituals in the history of
the human race is closed to us, it is possible to observe the entry
of human beings into the ritual and symbolic worlds. When a
baby is born, the symbiosis with the mother is ended. It must

breathe immediately with its own lungs, it must be touched, held or cuddled and later it must be fed. These ordinary yet primordial actions are the genetic code of all future ritualisation. They will be taken up into an ever more complex process of ritual actions and interactions that will make and keep life human.

Erikson's approach

Eric Erikson's writings on what he calls 'the ontogony of ritualisation' in infants and children has been hugely influential. For him, behaviour may be classified as ritual if it is interpersonal, repetitive and is value-oriented. It is significant activity which takes place between persons who are in vital interaction with each other and it communicates meaning and value. Erikson's first example of ritualisation is the 'greeting ritual' between mother and infant (but it seems necessary to maintain that this is possible only because of the post-natal experiences mentioned above). The waking infant communicates his/her state to the mother who 'approaches him with smiling or worried concern, brightly or anxiously voicing some appellation, and goes into action: looking, feeling, sniffing, she discovers possible sources of discomfort and initiates services to be rendered by rearranging the infant's position, by picking him up and so on. This daily event is highly ritualised, in that the mother seems to feel obliged, and not a little pleased, to repeat a performance arousing in the infant predictable responses which in turn encourage her to proceed.'[5] He points out that this behaviour is both highly individual and strongly stereotypical. It is the free, yet predictable and prescribed behaviour of this mother and this infant and yet is typical of mothers and infants. The interaction is obviously based on physical and biological need, yet the personal and emotional needs of the actants are also being fulfilled.

The pattern by which the mother and infant initiate mutual communication comprise sense stimuli and recognition rituals – a smell, a touch, a face, a voice, a smile, a name. Through such rituals their individual separateness is transcended, yet their distinctiveness is confirmed. By achieving this secure identification-in-separation, the basis for coping with the polarities of human life is being set down. The opposing but related experiences of presence and absence, dependence and autonomy, instinct and culture, separateness and unity, distinctiveness and integration, joy and tears, which characterise all human life, are already being faced through these rituals. They are playful yet formalised, familiar yet full of surprises. Through these ritual interchanges the infant's need for 'regular and mutual affirmation' is being addressed. The fundamentals of mutual recognition and affirmation rituals are being established in these exchanges. All future ritualisation during the person's life-span will seek ever new and more extensive enactment of these fundamentals.

The distinctive element of these rituals between mother and infant is described by Erikson as 'the numinous'. He maintains that all subsequent personality development in the person is dependent on the adequacy with which these foundational experiences and rituals are appropriated. Each new stage of growth builds on and recapitulates the earlier stages. The new subsumes and reinforces the values of the previous stage, so that they are simultaneously present to enrich and transform human life. Inadequate engagement in and appropriation of this stage of the process may inhibit the child's ability to successfully negotiate the complex demands of later stages. Such failure may give rise to anti-rituals like thumb-sucking, body-rocking, head-banging or bed-wetting.

He then passes on to the developments of early childhood which bring much greater mobility and more complex psychological development. At that stage, the child learns through ritualising behaviour to differentiate between acceptable and unacceptable behaviour, to be clear about what s/he is not to become (negative identity). In the process, the child must learn to cope with the demands, rules, boundaries, rewards (and punishments) that come from parents. The distinctive element here he names as the 'judicious'.

At the 'play age', the ritualisations of play with the peer group highlight the importance of imagination, creativity, initiative, and the dramatic in the child's life. With these gifts comes the possibility of constructing a world and rituals of his/her own. This enables a certain necessary distancing from 'numinous' parent-figures to take place. The 'play age' is also the stage at which children begin to piece together a coherent 'worldview', to inhabit alternatives in fantasy and, through ritual, to resolve the conflicts they experience.

At school, the child is introduced to the 'formal' dimension of ritualisation, where play is transformed into work and games into co-operation. Techniques and methods and competition become important in achieving what he calls 'competence'.

Adolescence brings together and stabilises the elements of ritualisation that have been internalised so far, into a higher synthesis of their own that seeks powerful ritual expression. The conflicting perceptions of them held by significant adults can generate an identity crisis for young people. They become easily disenchanted with the values and goals of the adult world and, with idealistic energy, they desire to co-construct a utopian alternative. There is a clear and enacted recognition of the need for collaboration with others in that project, what Erikson calls 'solidarity of conviction'. This ritualisation of belonging ensures that the vital affective element of ritual is internalised.

Towards the end of adolescence, 'rituals or rites of passage' become important. These rituals facilitate the transition from adolescence to adulthood and to definite acceptable authority roles within the culture. This 'solidarity of conviction' with what is regarded as important for adults in society, is achieved and people and communities are bonded together. Such rituals help to consolidate adult life once 'its commitments and investments have led to the creation of new persons and to the production of new things and ideas.'(112)

Of course, ritualisation does not cease when a person becomes adult. The meaning, values, attitudes, stability, sense of order and orientation, resolution of polar oppositions which have been developing cumulatively since infancy, must be reinforced and further developed through ongoing engagement with ritual, or what Erikson calls 're-ritualisation'.

Erikson's exposition of the role of ritual in the development and integration of the human person, helps us to appreciate that ritual is not an optional extra in life. From the rituals of 'mutual recognition' to those which promote 'solidarity of convictions', we see how indispensable it is in the process of personalising, socialising and humanising, in making and keeping life human. If what ritual alone can mediate is only inadequately present in the lives of human beings, they will face psychological conflict and estrangement from self and society.

The need for ritual
This absolute need for ritual, from a psychological and

developmental point of view, is solidly confirmed from social
and cultural perspectives by the research of many sociologists
and anthropologists. They agree that ritual is ineradicable from
human life. It mediates the worldview or meaning-system of a
culture or social group; it sustains and nourishes social structures; it facilitates social coherence and group bonding; it mid-
wifes social change and cultural transformation; it can challenge
the group to examine the consistency between what is enacted
ritually and what is lived daily; between what is and what it
should be. Without ritual, human culture and society could not
survive.

Yet despite this massive endorsement of the ritual character of
life, and the absolute need that human beings have for ritual,
some people are still inclined to dismiss ritual as 'irrelevant' to
their lives, as 'empty' or 'meaningless'. Ritual, as we have seen,
is so much part of life, so essential to life, yet they find it difficult
to perceive its all-pervasive influence. They rest happy with 'the
way things are' and reject ritual without realising that what is
being taken for granted is itself the product of ritualisation. It is
difficult to see ritual as the rhythm at the heart of life and of the
struggle to be human. Life is founded on ritual and we live
immersed in ritual as fish in water but as someone remarked,
whoever discovered water it wasn't fish!

If we doubt the significance of ritual in the life of human beings,
we should consider taking part in a wedding ceremony and see
how insistent people are that all aspects of the ritual be fulfilled.
In marriage, the bonds of loyalty to parents and family are transcended and the bride and groom define themselves publicly as
a couple, as a new family unit. This brings about a change in the
entire set of relations between them and all those who know
them. This deep and lasting transition is so significant that it demands the mediation of ritual, and all those who take part in it
know that instinctively. We can think too of the elaborate secular rituals associated with politics, sport, law courts, schools,
theatre, universities, advertising, etc. We remember how spontaneously people resort to ritual in times of crisis or tragedy. We
recall how ritual helps people through the stages of bereave-
ment. We wonder what we would do without greeting rituals –
whether simple or more formal (and we know how awkward
we feel if the smoothness of that simple ritual is changed in any

way). It seems that, at another time, the grasping of the right hand – the dagger hand – signified mutual distrust, whereas in the present convention it signifies trust and welcome. The action is exactly the same, but the content is radically different.

What ritual does

Human beings have always had to face the bewildering complexity of life, the mystery of evil, of suffering, of death, and have responded by searching for meaning, wholeness, 'salvation' in the broadest sense. And every meaning-system has claimed to offer an answer by binding the past, present and future of the individual to the memories and hopes, the stories and rituals that are basic to the life and identity of that system. From the moment the symbiosis between foetus and mother ends at birth, rituals are needed to cope with the symbolic distance between them. It is through the body, and rituals involving the body, that we express ourselves in relation to the other. Those embodied rituals become more complex as the questions about the relatedness of self and non-self become more acute. The life-long question: How can I be myself and relate to the other/s or the group or society or history?, can be addressed satisfactorily only through ritual – interpersonal and communal. It is through ritual that the associated perennial questions about how the self is related to the now and the no-longer-now, the now and the not–yet, the now and the not-merely-now, are actively resolved.

Human beings have an extraordinary ability to turn actions and gestures into rituals so that they can dig down into the depths of human experience and communicate with each other about the mysterious paradoxes of life. They have the potential to express ritually what lies too deep for words, 'when words after speech reach into silence'. (Eliot) Ritual can bring to birth what still remains when language ceases or is at best only a stammer. It may indeed become the 'language' of the unthinkable that must yet be lived through. How can we communicate the realities of suffering and death, of love and fear, hope and despair, of agony and ecstasy, the limit-experiences in the 'dream-crossed twilight between birth and dying' (Eliot)? 'Not everything has a name ... lost between awe and wonder we find no words to say ...' (Tolkien) We need the total language that ritual is, to speak about the greatness and littleness of human beings. Ritual can illuminate, interpret and unify the experiences of our lives that are most profound, most rich but also most incommunicable. Without ritual, so much of these experiences would remain mute, destructive and ultimately unbearable. Ritual is what people do when words are not enough – whether it is a symbolic action with scarves at the time of the Hillsborough tragedy, or with yellow ribbons or tee-shirts for very different kinds of victories or the candles for hostages or dustbin lids for internment or ...

Ritual, narrative and symbol

We might at this stage attempt an unnuanced generalisation about the interrelatedness of ritual, narrative and symbol. A narrative is often defined as a recital of events. A myth is a type of narrative which purports to speak of 'events' beyond time and which communicates truths so fundamental to human life that they can only be expressed in the language of symbols. Story is usually understood as a type of narrative about characters and events, recognisable as being within our time and space. Through the creative power of imagination, human beings can go intuitively to the heart of the raw, unedited experiences of life and transpose them into integrating narrative. They can evoke, narrate and retell the story until the pattern of words becomes commensurate with the inner meaning, the human significance of the experience. But the story always carries a 'surplus of meaning', it is multivocal, and is patient of ever-deeper exploration that defies reduction to conceptual abstraction. The story itself draws on memory, imagination, ritual and symbol, yet despite the extraordinary power of narrative, human communication tends beyond words towards enactment.

The ritual dynamism implicit (or at times explicit) in the story demands appropriate expression in behaviour that is interpersonal, repetitive and adaptive (characteristics which it shares with story). What is first experienced and then transposed into powerful narrative, is now enacted ritually. Ritual is 'engendered by experience' (Ricoeur) and facilitates contact with the significance of that experience through its own unique mediation. Because so much is compressed into the ritual action, we can understand something of the extraordinary, supercharged power of ritual.

A symbol can be understood as the smallest unit of ritual which still maintains within itself the essence of the ritual process. (See

V. Turner, *Dramas, Fields and Metaphors*, Cornell U. Press, 1974).
Ritual can then be seen as a bundle of interacting symbols which
again evoke and embody much more than can be articulated
logically. They speak of the heart of things and speak to our
hearts. Again because so much is condensed into symbolic ritual,
there is a need for some appropriate narration if their range of
reference is to be focused. The appropriateness of these interpretative words needs to be highlighted because of the constant
temptation to destroy ritual by trying to reduce it to words only
(a temptation not always resisted by liturgical presiders).
Appropriate ritual language must reach down into the mystery
of life and, through the power of metaphor, seek to disclose
something of the depth of meaning that the ritual is communicating in another medium. Such language must be capable of
multiple significance and reference, it must encompass feelings,
values and meaning. It is at its most powerful when it is able to
trigger imaginatively a chain-reaction of interacting symbols.

Symbol

The English word *symbol* is derived from the Greek *symbolon*,
and even in translation it still preserves something of the Greek
love of dialogue and dialectic. Its parent verb *synballein* means to
bring or to throw together, to unite, to match, to dovetail, to
tally. The distinguishable elements that come together may be
similar, in which case symbolisation involves steadily creating
an organic whole; or dissimilar so that their conjunction is surprising, innovative and challenging. Considered in itself, a *symbolon* is a broken, incomplete entity somehow calling out for
completion, signifying wholeness. Its very incompleteness implies the existence of its other part which is, as it were, 'given
and not given' with itself. Two halves of a broken coin, each
called a *symbolon*, could be exchanged between contracting par-
ties, each part implying the other with its duties and responsibil-
ities. A soldier's badge of allegiance or a messenger's token of
authorisation or a watchman's token of identity, could also be
called a *symbolon*. A departing guest might be given a potsherd
by her host and she in turn might give that *symbolon* to a friend
of hers. That person would then be guaranteed the same hospi-
tality when the potsherd she now possessed as a token of identity
tallied with that of the host.

The significance of such customs is taken up and developed to
interpret the mysterious reality of human love in Plato's

Symposium. Aristophanes recounts the myth of the Androgyne – that originally human beings were composite, circular beings who possessed the characteristics of both genders. But they became too proud, too self-sufficient and as punishment they were cut in half by Zeus and, after minor surgical adjustments, were launched into the world. He concludes: 'It is from this distant epoch, then, that we may date the innate love which human beings feel for one another, the love which restores us to our ancient state by attempting to weld two beings into one and to heal the wounds which humanity suffered. Each of us is the symbol or broken tally of a human being ... and each of us is perpetually in search of our corresponding tally or symbol.'

In the early Christian centuries, the baptismal profession of faith was referred to as the *symbolum fidei* because it distinguished the Christian from the non-Christian and it created and expressed mutual recognition and unity among Christians. Each person was understood to hold the faith only as *symbolon*, only as a broken and incomplete reality which could only attain unity and completeness when it tallied and dovetailed with the faith of the community. Even the faith of the church itself was thought to have this symbol character because it must refer beyond itself constantly to *the* source of truth. For the theological teachers and writers of that time, mystery, symbol and sacrament were virtually interchangeable. That link weakened substantially over the centuries but it was not completely lost to sight. Although some of the Reformers were using symbol in weakened sense, the Council of Trent in its decree on the eucharist taught that: 'The most Holy Eucharist has indeed this in common with the other sacraments that it is a symbol of a sacred thing and a visible form of an invisible grace'. (D 1639)

Definition

How are we to define symbol? There are almost as many definitions of symbol as there are writers on symbol. We will select two of them from writings spanning a twenty-five-year period. 'A symbol, in general, is a relatively stable and repeatable element of perceptual experience, standing for some larger meaning or set of meanings which cannot be given or not fully given, in perceptual experience itself.'[6] 'A symbol is a complex of gestures, sounds, images, and/or words, that evoke, invite, and persuade participation in that to which they refer.'[7]

How symbols work

The affinity between these definitions and the description of ritual is noteworthy. Both definitions remind us that symbols do not exist simply for their own sake, they are not 'that which, but that through which' (Ricoeur). Symbols belong to the world of human meaning, of value, of affectivity, of communication and communion. Those who interact with them are involved intellectually, emotionally and ethically. Symbols may facilitate either the weaving of meaning into an organic whole or precipitate a leap to a new level of meaning. Symbols always communicate a surplus of meaning, so they constantly invite further interaction and deeper exploration. Yet it would be wrong to think of this happening in some kind of extrinsic way, for symbols participate in the reality which they symbolise. The meaning, the value, the communion, is realised and recognised in and through the otherness of the symbol. Symbols speak, draw and seek to unite so that you cannot be indifferent to symbol as symbol once it is recognised. (The parallels between this sequence and the *sacramentum tantum, res et sacramentum* and *res tantum* of traditional sacramental theology is interesting.) Symbols enable us to interpret, express and transform experience, and in the process they are experienced as active, even alive. They are engendered by experience and offer it in another mediation. They can open up, illuminate, interpret and unify dimensions of human experience that we could not reach otherwise. But they can never exhaust the experience or encapsulate the mystery, so there can never be a complete identity between symbol and reality (or else we would simply have the reality itself). On the other hand, there cannot be a division between symbol and reality either for then we would be left with a mere pointer. This has led some authors to distinguish sharply between sign and symbol. Sign is presented as having a clear, one-to-one relationship to the reality which it designates by convention for our convenience. Symbol by contrast is not created arbitrarily but is 'engendered by experience', born out of tradition. It enjoys a many-to-many relationship with the reality symbolised and is concerned with the meaning and the ultimacy of life. But this distinction should not be pressed too far, for the symbol must have the function of signification and what appears as functional may yield an unsuspected depth of significance.

At any rate, the question should alert us to the mysterious yet fragile and ambivalent relationship between symbol and reality, of unity-in-distinction, of identity and non-identity, of presence and absence, of revealing and veiling, of is and is not. Yet this fragility and ambivalence is the symbol's strength for it means that it will not draw attention to itself ('not that which') but invites the interplay of memory, imagination, intuition and transformation. To the dismissive remark 'it's only a symbol' our response might be, there *are* only symbols.

Organic growth

Erikson, we remember, believed that it was necessary to describe as numinous the distinctive element of the mutual recognition rituals between mother and infant, especially the infant's response to the her as a hallowed presence. This numinous quality experienced in and through the body should, he believed, be an indispensable element in all ritual-making but he recognised that it would be most obvious within religious rituals. There 'the result is a sense of separateness transcended, and yet also of distinctiveness confirmed and thus of the very basis of a sense of "I" renewed (as it feels) by the mutual recognition of all "I's" joined in a shared faith in one all-embracing "I am".'[8] His approach also alerts us to the existence of different stages of ritualisation among worshippers. It also raises questions about how these stages might be related to what is expressed in liturgical celebrations. Such convictions should help us to realise that our religious rituals are not imposed arbitrarily but that they grow organically out of life.

Basis for Sacraments

It was suggested earlier that it might be possible to go back behind even the rituals of mutual recognition acknowledged by Erikson and found the basis for all ritualisation in the breath, embrace and feeding of the new born. Might it not be possible also to locate the ultimate basis for the experience of the numinous in those experiences? It seems permissible to link the religious rituals of the Judaeo-Christian tradition to those elemental experiences of breathing, bonding and assimilating. We will be attending to Israel's tradition in a moment, but first a suggestion as to how we might establish that link with our seven sacraments.

Despite a gnostic and docetic tendency within our tradition to down-play the involvement of the body in sacramental worship, we must remember that our sacraments exist for embodied people. We name them as nouns but they are ritual actions that involve anointing, feeding, touching, embracing embodied human beings. It is difficult to see how such gestures would not evoke, at some level, our very first experiences and their developing complexification. Could we not see baptism as the gift of the life-giving breath/spirit of the crucified/risen Lord; confirmation as the embrace of full acceptance into the community; eucharist as consuming the body and blood of the Lord so that we are assimilated to him; penance as the reconciling embrace; anointing of the sick as the strengthening and healing embrace (or in some cases the final embrace); order as the embrace of commissioning to ministry on behalf of the community; marriage as the passionate and life-giving embrace.

Within Israel

Within Israel, the word we translate as 'spirit' originally meant 'air in motion', especially the wind or breath. These mysterious sources of energy and life were understood as manifestations of God's creative power. So in time God was spoken of as active in creation through God's breath/spirit which moved 'over the face of the waters' (Gen 1:2) and God is said to create life by breathing into the dust of the earth 'the breath of life'. (Gen 2:7) Spirit as breath was understood to in-spire (literally, breath through) gifted people who enhanced the life of God's people – leaders and heroes, sages and prophets, poets and social reformers, people of insight and foresight, preachers and writers. Together they gave us the story of the people wrestling with evil, experiencing suffering, exile, death, and questing for meaning, hope, salvation, wholeness, solidarity, humanity. They were the people who gave us the magnificent vision of God's salvific graciousness outlined in chapter five. It was story, symbol and ritual that overcame divisions, bonded them together as a people and promised and enacted the most intimate union between God and the people. In the book of Jeremiah, Yahweh is presented as saying 'I was thinking how I would number you among my sons and daughters ... I was thinking how you would call me, my father, and would not turn from following me.' (3:19) God's desire to ingather his sons and daughters is what the bible sees as holding together everything from the creation to the consummation of the world. Human beings according to the biblical vision are creatures created in the image and likeness of God, called to be the image of God, called to be eternally ingathered (we remember that according to John, Jesus died 'to gather together in unity the scattered children of God' (11:52) and in the third Eucharistic Prayer we say 'from age to age you gather a people to yourself'.) We see this theme working itself out in the history of Israel through the stories, rituals and symbols that lie at the heart of her identity as a people. Revelation, election, covenant, assembly and *zikkaron* are central to that identity.

In a simplified and abbreviated code, we could speak of revelation in action and interpretative word, in the history of Israel, and she experienced this as an invitation to respond in action and word. That revelation, she believed, identified God as offering love and communion to her, and graciously initiating an intimate relationship. That Yahweh who created Israel should relate to her as a chosen 'thou' can only be 'explained' in terms of love – 'the Lord set his love on you and chose you' (Deut 7) and 'from among all the families of the earth I have known only you'. (Amos 3:2) This election seeks a free response – 'choose whom you will serve' (Jos 24:15), 'today I put before you the way of life and the way of death'. (Deut 30:15, Jer 21:8) The invitation and the response are summed up in the refrain 'I will be your God and you will be my people' which recalls the marriage formula. It also articulates in summary form the mutual agreements and obligations implied in the *covenant*. We note the rituals with altar, pillars, sacrifice, that accompany the establishment of the covenant in Exodus 24:1-11 and the ritual word – 'all that the Lord has spoken we will do'. (7) Even more surprising is the never-to-be-repeated prophetic action of throwing half the blood of the sacrificed animals against the altar and half on the people, with the interpretative word 'behold the blood of the covenant which the Lord has made with you ...' (8) This symbolises that the closest possible relationship exists between God and the people, a blood relationship. God is next-of-kin. Finally, we have eating and drinking in the presence of the Lord.

Although there is no formal covenant festival as such, we remember the many symbols by which the covenant was recalled – the Ark, standing stones, the tent of meeting, circumcision, Passover, etc. The recall of Exodus and the covenant relationship gathered the unedited fragments of history and their daily story into a coherent whole. It explicitated what was mute and obscure in their experience. It enlightened the darkness of sorrow and pain and it kindled hopes for the present and the future in the vibrant memory of the past. Even when she repeatedly broke the covenant and rejected the stipulation that her election was for service to justice, Israel never quite forgot her identity as a covenanted people, called to closer union and deeper communion with God. She was reminded forcefully of her vocation when she gathered in assembly around a representative of God to hear the word of God – the creative word that can shatter the rock. (Jer 23:29) Yahweh had promised to 'live and move among them and be their God and they shall be my people'(Lev 26:12) and this presence was mediated in palpable ways through the liturgical assembly. There the recital of God's saving actions and their ritual enactment mediate the power and will of Yahweh.

Israel's ritual forms did not fall ready-made from heaven nor did she invent radically new rituals. Rather she took up and used what was available in history and culture. But while the external forms may remain relatively unchanged, and therefore ambiguous at the level of gesture, the interpretive word makes it clear that they now refer only to the saving action of Yahweh. Killing and eating a lamb, baking and eating unleavened bread from the first sheaves of the harvest, could take place among many peoples and among many religious traditions. But through the mediation of the ritual word it was clear that for Israel they had been historicised, Yahwehised. Yet we should not think of this recital as a bland unchanging repetition. We have plenty of evidence for a prophetic remembrance that confronted the people with the inescapable significance of their core-story and the demands of integral worship. But they also confronted Israel's core-story with the trials, the sufferings, the calamities endured by the people and, in the process, engaged creatively with the stories, ritual and symbols of the tradition.

Zikkaron

When Israel celebrated the Passover ritual for example, when they ate the passover lamb, chewed the bitter herbs and stood staff in hand, they were convinced that Yahweh was as really present and active among them as among their ancestors on the night they were led out of Egypt. 'It is you who came out of Egypt ... I brought you out of Egypt.' (Deut 16:1-7) The key to this conviction is given in the command: 'This day shall be for you a memorial day (*Le-Zikkaron*) and you shall celebrate it as a feast in Yahweh's honour.' (Ex 12:14) The Hebrew, *zikkaron* (*azkarah*) is usually translated as *anamnesis* in Greek and as *memorial* or *remembrance* in English, but neither host language can do justice to its full range of meaning. They can only imply a recollection of the past in the present whereas *zikkaron* seeks to conjoin past, present and future, to combine memory and action and to make present events and persons. Behind this rich concept lies the biblical insight into the nature of human memory and the conviction about God's relationship to time. From experience they knew that they could hold together in memory, past, present and future. To remember is to be in touch with the links between the now and the not-merely-now and to be in communion with the only constant in all of this, the One who sustains it all. That insight could convince them that what they regarded as past, present and future were equally and actively compresent to God as the one who creates, sustains and brings to completion. God's eternity is the fullness of time (not timelessness as in Greek thinking) and what is experienced by human beings in time is moving toward a God-willed fulfilment and completion. God's deeds in history took place not merely for those immediately involved but for all the people and for each succeeding generation. It is this conviction that the core of God's action has perduring power and can be an actuality in story and ritual for succeeding generations, that is the foundation of their liturgies. The depths of meaning in the concept are still being plumbed by scholars but what has already been uncovered has brought extraordinary riches to our appreciation of liturgy and to ecumenical understandings as well. On-going efforts to link it with the covenant relationship and to explore further the power of symbol, imagination and prophetic remembrance, will no doubt bear further fruit.

We will leave the last word to a prayer from the *Passover Haggadah*,[9] which illustrates Israel's desire to remember and praise in assembly for the grace of election.

'The breath of all the living is praise of You, O God.
The spirit of all the flesh is Your eternal glory, O our King.
From everlasting to everlasting You are God.
And beside You, we have no sovereign, no redeemer.

Were our mouths as full of song as the sea
And our tongues with melody as the multitude of its waves,
Our eyes shining like the sun and the moon,
Our arms like soaring eagles' pinions,
Our limbs like those of the swift gazelle,
Still our power would be nought to show
The thousand myriad bounties You have bestowed
Upon our fathers and on us.

But, O God, limbs and tongue and heart and mind,
Join now to praise You Name,
As every tongue will yet avow You
And every soul give You allegiance.

As it it written: All my bones shall shout in joy:
O God, who is like You?

And as David sang:
Praise the Lord, my whole being!
All that is within me:
Praise His Holy Name!'

Notes:

1. Sheed and Ward, 1963.

2. Herder, 1963.

3. *Theology Digest*, 19:3, Autumn, 1971.

4. Chesterton, G.K., *Heretics*, 97

5. *Toys and Reasons: Stages in the ritualisation of experience*, W.W. Norton, 1977.

6. Wheelwright, Philip, *Metaphor and Reality*, Indiana University Press, 1962, 92

7. *Symbol*, Stephen Happel, N.D.T., Gill and MacMillian, 1987.

8. *Toys and Reasons*, 90

9. Central Conference of American Rabbis, Penguin Books, 1982.

CHAPTER 9

Jesus and the eucharist

'In a crumb of bread the whole mystery is.'
Patrick Kavanagh

In this final chapter we will review the life and ministry of Jesus of Nazareth as the source for Christian praxis and praise. We will pay particular attention to what should be allowed to challenge and transform both our living and celebration.

Filling out the images
Christian disciples are women and men who believe that Jesus Christ is 'the Way, the Truth and the Life'. (Jn 14:16) Disciples have always fleshed out the content of the words 'Jesus Christ' (or explained why they believe in him) by drawing on some image of him from the many available within the tradition, and then elaborating on it. Our own first associations with that name were no doubt established in childhood and deepened through experience and schooling. Through the years, our dominant image of him may have changed many times but never by way of a simple replacement of one image by another. The whole set of images that charter our ongoing efforts from childhood to this moment to appreciate something of the mystery of Jesus Christ, are always simultaneously available to us. So we must wrestle with all of that rich variety each time we seek to regain the image of him that now seems most appropriate and most consistent with the New Testament writings and with our present complex experience. We may be heartened when we remember that this process of imaging and re-imaging Jesus Christ in our lives is a pale reflection of the vibrant process of renaming Jesus that characterised the early Christian communities. The extraordinary character of that process is brought home to us as we remember that there are forty-two new images or titles for the Risen One in the pages of the New Testament, and no doubt many others that we cannot recognise. We may remember too

the amazing variety and contrariety of images of Jesus Christ
found in the history of Christian art forms.

It seems that Christians have never been content with the mere
recitation of the credal formulae about Christ. Their foundational
faith in him sought to express itself above all in the kind of lives
they lived. True faith must first and foremost be practical and
performative; it is a way of living. However they also felt the
need to give expression to their personal faith in him by drawing
on the master images of Christ which were available within the
culture and theology of any given time or place. It could not be
otherwise, for in proclaiming their faith in Christ, Christians are
not called merely to give intellectual assent to a set of propositions or engage in some activity of the mind. 'I believe,' *Credo*,
comes from *cor dare*, to set my heart on, to give my heart and
hopes to. It calls for commitment of the whole person, for a loving response from the whole person, with whole heart, whole
soul, whole mind. The root image behind the word 'person' is
'what sounds through' me as I speak or act. So in saying 'I believe in Jesus Christ' I am endeavouring to gather the whole web
of relationships and relatedness that makes me what I am, into
engagement with all I believe him to be. As St Thomas Aquinas
reminds us, 'the act of the believer does not terminate with the
proposition but in the reality'. (S.T. II-II Q, la 2ad 2)

Obviously then, believers would need to know more of this person than what is offered by the creeds – his name, his lineage, a
few titles given to him by the early communities and some facts
about his last days. Strangely, what is not mentioned in the
creeds – the life, the message and ministry of Jesus Christ – becomes indispensable. Most people today feel the need to go back
behind creeds and councils into contact with the faith of the
New Testament communities. It should then be possible, they
believe, to come into contact with the foundation of that faith in
the life and ministry, death and new life of Jesus the Christ.

Truly human
In this undertaking, Roman Catholics are able to draw on the
fruits of over forty years of theological and biblical scholarship
which has struggled to recover the scriptural foundations of our
faith. In particular, they can benefit from the renewed insights
into the full, integral humanity of Jesus Christ which have characterised much of that scholarship. Through the work of these

scholars, it has become possible to fill out the bare bones of the credal statements about Christ in an exciting way and to restore its full meaning to the phrase 'truly human' (from Chalcedon's creed).

It has been a long and difficult struggle, however, to rectify the overstress on the divinity of Christ at the expense of his humanity which characterised classical christology. The creeds, which pass over the life and ministry of Jesus of Nazareth, could do little to overcome that imbalance. And since the themes for much preaching were drawn from that creed, the humanity of Jesus Christ did not gain its rightful place in the minds and imaginations of Roman Catholics. The rosary too reinforced that same pattern, passing immediately as it does, from the joyful mysteries of his conception, birth and youth to the sorrowful mysteries.

Given the weight of that tradition, even when people in the past spoke of the incarnation of Christ, the one-sided stress on the divine nature of the incarnate word was so strong that they sailed close to the heresy of Apollinarianism.

In the 1960s and 70s, some people managed to move beyond that position as they tried to take seriously the new insights into the humanity of Jesus Christ which had been emerging in scripture studies and theology. Since they believed that God became human in Jesus Christ, it became important for them to know as much as possible about the kind of human being he became. We might suspect, though, that some of them still saw themselves as making a difficult act of faith in his divinity and then proving the fact of his humanity – that he was tired, hungry, angry and so on. It was as if they had to prove that he had enough of what they recognised in themselves and in others to justify saying that he was 'truly human'. That new position was hard won and was difficult to maintain consistently, especially when questions were raised about his knowledge, his sinlessness or his sexuality.

Today all of us are being challenged to go further still. We are asked to realise that confessing the humanity of Jesus Christ means making a true act of faith in him in the fullest sense, an act of faith which can only enhance our faith in his divinity. It means proclaiming that he is our Lord because he is 'Son of Man', the truly human one, the 'Second Adam' through whom the human race is reconstituted. It is not a matter of showing that he possessed at least the minimum requirements for solidarity with humanity as we know it. Rather, through knowing him we are being invited to set out in quest of a humanity whose existence we hardly suspect. To believe in Jesus Christ means accepting his way as the only pattern and model and guide for our lives, for our quest for humanity. (See *Gaudium et Spes* 22, *Redemptor Hominis* 8.) It means responding to him because he reveals the humanity that lies dormant in all of us, overlaid with apathy and self-protectiveness. It means acknowledging the call of a humanity which we usually stifle lest it awaken us to the way of passionate discipleship. It means cherishing the humanity we fear.[1]

The link between belief in Jesus Christ and human flourishing, however, cannot be taken for granted as obvious. At the end of the second century, the philosopher Celsus rejected Christianity as inhuman and ridiculed its founder, its message, its praxis and its adherents as unworthy of God. How could anything human derive from the crucified one and his cross? Down the centuries, others have echoed his sentiments and accused Christians of justifying the inhuman, canonising poverty and suffering, and killing the joy of human well-being in the name of the cross of Christ. Some have even maintained that if human beings are to be fully human, God and his crucified Christ must be rejected.

Many Christians who would oppose such positions, nevertheless wonder what they can say about the struggle to be human at the end of a century that has witnessed the massive inhumanity of battlefields and Gulags, Auschwitz and Hiroshima. How can we believe in humanity when human beings are destroying the life of the planet itself, when discrimination, neo-colonisation, torture, the nuclear threat are part of state polity? How can we speak of a new way of being human, or profess our faith in a saviour, in a world where a billion human beings are forced to live in absolute poverty with its attendant horrors of needless hunger, suffering, disease, homelessness and premature death? Do the negativities of human existence today not mock all tentative discourse about 'humanity?' Is the credibility of Christianity itself not on trial?

Back to the ministry and message
In the face of such questions the impulse, noted above, to look again, critically, at the message and ministry of Jesus of Nazareth

becomes all the more pressing. We need to rediscover his basic credo, what it was he gave his heart to, what his spirituality was, what stand he took for the good of human beings in the world of his time. Not that this will give us an instant blueprint for what we need to do in the changed circumstances of today, but it will put us in touch with what should inspire, inform and critique our own discipleship of Jesus Christ, our quest for the humanity he revealed to us.

We may begin by asking: What was the credo of Jesus of Nazareth? What vision inspired him? What did he live for? What was he prepared to die for? Why was he considered dangerous? Who was for him? Who was against him?

The credo, the vision, the goal and the strategy that lies behind all that he says and does is the kingdom or reign of God. In order to appreciate what he meant by the kingdom/reign of God, we must keep in mind constantly his hearers with whom he is interacting. And to understand his hearers we must try to appreciate the complex, interwoven, social, religious, political and economic circumstances of that time. It is to these hearers, in these circumstances, that Jesus proclaims the kingdom of God, and by that proclamation he seeks to change both hearers and circumstance.

Roman domination brought its own share of oppression and anguish to the people, but the formalism and sectarianism which characterised the religious system of that time took an even greater toll on the socially and religiously marginalised. The religious elite had decided on the criteria that granted access to God's grace and then, believing that their criteria were divinely sanctioned, proceeded to ostracise 'the poor and the sinner'. Those who were actually poor and those whose way of life was judged to be sinful, were declared to be cut off from God and from salvation. The consequences of such an inhuman judgement were far more devastating than anything the Romans could ever do, for they struck at the very roots of these people's 'humanity' and robbed them of the hope of a future. And the 'poor and the sinners' accepted this judgement of their religious 'superiors' fatalistically, though no doubt they saw in it a reflection of the inhumanity of God. The judgement condemned them to eternal failure and threatened to stamp out the spark of humanity within them as it drove them to the edge of despair.

It is not difficult to see that these unfortunate people were being dehumanised by others, but we must also recognise that in the process the oppressors were destroying their own humanity too. We must think of humanity as interwoven, realise that we are truly 'one body', and understand that what happens to the part happens to the whole.

Kingdom/reign of God

In that situation, Jesus proclaims the kingdom/reign of God, a profoundly social symbol which for centuries had summed up the quintessence of Israel's hopes and longings for salvation. For his hearers, this symbol would have functioned by evoking the complex of stories and rituals which celebrated the great things that God had done in their history for the whole people. It was this symbolic complex that gave them their identity as a people and their hopes for the future. When Jesus proclaims this symbol, it will be heard as referring to a real transformation of social and historical reality on behalf of the whole people. It evokes the dream that God has for the world and its history, and God's presence and action to make that dream a reality. Obviously then, it is going to be God's work, but the crucial question then and now is: The reign of *which* God? It is his unique understanding of the God of that kingdom that differentiates Jesus' proclamation from that of others. He passionately insists on portraying God as the author of life, as the lover of humanity whose dream is for what is best for all God's daughters and sons, 'that they might have life and have it to the full'. (Jn 10:10) The coming of this God would not strike terror in the hearts of the 'poor and the sinners'. This God is the God who loves us into existence, who cherishes us absolutely in existence and awaits our free response to this unconditional initiative, who loves us in life and death with a love stronger than death. Over and over again he speaks of a God who is utterly gracious, compassionate and merciful. This is a God who is unconditional in love and prodigal in forgiveness, a God who 'hugs humanity into his very self'. (G. Herbert) The kingdom comes purely from God's love. It cannot be precipitated by violence or merited through strict, legal observance or accessed through the rituals of sacrifice.

Negatively, Jesus' prophetic preaching implies that much of what exists within the holiness system is contrary to God's reign, to his dream of fullness of life for all. The kingdom/reign of God, since it is for life and against death, must assert itself against the anti-kingdom. So he has to unmask the false deities which, while rejoicing in honourable names, destroyed the humanity of even their own devotees. He must struggle against all that is anti-kingdom in all its devious ways, against all that is suffused by death.

At the beginning of his ministry, Luke tells us, Jesus sets himself against all that diminishes humanity in any way and throughout his ministry he remains faithful to that charter. The presence and action of the Holy One was to be discerned in what enhanced the life of all and opposed death in all its forms.

Prayer

The gospels make it clear that his ministry is rooted in constant prayer and may hint at the mystical quality of that prayer. Jesus will allow no obstacles or barriers, however sacred they may seem to be, to come between God and the one who prays. He bridged the unfathomable gap maintained in Jewish piety between God and human beings at prayer, and in an act of unparalleled intimacy he renamed that God, Abba, the loving father constantly accessible to all his daughters and sons. But we should note that he did not find all forms of prayer compatible with God's reign and he warns against inauthentic prayer. This man of prayer is forever active in the thick of life, dedicated to crucifying service to other people. He is forever struggling with them and for them so that the new vision he is proposing may become theirs. He is struggling to change their basic credo, their foundational spirituality.

Parables

That vision is communicated in a powerful and subversive way through his parables. He tells stories about characters who act in surprising ways because of a dream that they have, because of something that is precious to them beyond all else. Through the imaginative interplay generated by these stories, which can turn the hearers' world upside down and inside out, they are asked: Can you imagine human relations being transformed like that? If you can, then you have caught a glimpse of the dream that God has for the world, of a new way of being human together.

Into the tortured history of conflict between Jews and Samaritans, Jesus tells a story which allows his audience to experience imag-

inatively the gift of life coming from a traditional enemy. The
basis for this action is not kith or kin, or class or moral precept,
or love of God, but common humanity – 'the Samaritan when he
saw him had compassion'. He was able to enter into the pain of
the other, recognising that he too had emerged from the one
womb of common humanity. In the story of the Prodigal, we re-
joice that the younger son, who had become a gentile according
to the strict letter of the law, has his life, his human dignity and
sonship restored to him. But we remember that the humanity of
the father was also at risk. Whatever the law may demand, you
cannot cut off your own flesh and blood without destroying
your own humanity. And what of the life and humanity of the
elder brother?

Good news to the poor
The shocking, scandalous and subversive character of Jesus'
proclamation of the kingdom, which is found in many of the
parables, is clearest when he preaches it as 'good news to the
poor'. Many of Jesus' contemporaries found it to be shocking
and scandalous and sought to silence him. Many Christians too
were soon shocked by it and set out to remove the scandal. They
tended to edit out these references to the poor and produce a
syncopated master-text of their own, a kind of bland fifth
gospel. We have inherited a tradition wherein the best minds
and most persuasive pens were at work to convince us that 'the
poor' in the gospels does not mean the materially, economically
or sociologically poor. Consequently it is very difficult for us to
hear what is being said to us in the name of God and of the poor.
That tradition told us that references to 'the poor' really meant
'the poor in spirit', which in turn was to be understood as those
who placed their trust in God and sought to be virtuous – hum-
ble, meek, merciful, pure in heart. Wealth and possessions were
quite compatible with these virtues ('Woe to you who are
wealthy' always seems to apply to someone else!) provided one's 'attitude' was right or one had a spirit of 'detachment' or was prepared, in carefully defined circumstances, to give part of their
superflua to a worthy cause, even to 'the deserving poor'! Such
an approach stretched the meaning of the word 'poor' until it
referred to the well-to-do rather than to those who were actually
poor!

Armed with this piece of non-sense, those who were poor could debate endlessly the definition of 'the poor' and conclude that the real poor were those 'who did not savour the things of God'; or 'who had lost the faith'; or who, while being affluent, had 'problems' in their lives or marriages or families; or were 'under pressure' from taxation or mortgages. Such problems should of course call forth compassion from us, but there are perfectly accurate words to describe any of these conditions without hijacking the word 'poor'. To use it with these inappropriate frames of reference is to oppress the poor to the point of depriving them of their very last possession – their name.

What the scriptures say

If we are to critique that tradition it will be necessary to hear the biblical resonances behind Jesus' preaching and action. Briefly, there are sixteen root words for different forms of oppression in the First Testament.[2] This massive vocabulary speaks of those who are bent over, distressed, wrongfully impoverished, humiliated by those who wish to amass wealth and possessions. It tells of those deprived of the necessities of life, those who go hungry, those who are destitute. *Ani'* is the word most frequently used to refer to such people and its root image is: being bent over, crushed, humiliated, 'being one of those whose power/ hand wavers.' (Lev 25:35) The Greek word *ptochos*, from the verb *ptosso*, to crouch or to bend down, is used to translate *ani'* and it refers to the economically afflicted, the dispossessed, the destitute. We must remember that 'poverty' and 'wealth' are not neutral or value-free terms. They are strictly correlated. In the bible, the word 'poor' is always judgemental; it calls for a taking of sides. It exposes the causal relationship between the poor and the wealthy 'who grind the face of the poor'. (Is 3:15) It names victims, denounces the consequences of oppression, reveals conflict, declares who God is and discerns where God's reign is to be found.

At the time of Jesus, the country, as we saw, was experiencing the consequences of external domination. But the structures of internal oppression created even greater burdens especially for the poorest and weakest who, as always, suffered most. The wealthy, who were also religiously and politically influential, created the poverty which laid the hand of death on the living. And there were very many poor people in Israel: widows, orphans, day labourers, the unemployable, lepers, beggars, 'the maimed, the blind and lame'. Furthermore, the condition of the poor was religiously sanctioned. In the judgement of the religious elite, they were poor because they were sinners. And the poor accepted this judgement fatalistically and resigned all hope of overcoming their poverty or of experiencing salvation.

This is the context of Jesus' ministry. In most of the gospel material we see Jesus interacting with the religious situation or questioning its structures and institutions. But because it is a holiness system, we must be alert also to the political implications of what he says and does.

As a system

It is possible to see that religious context as a system i.e. 'an organised whole of interrelated parts', and this may help to highlight the structural parallels between the situations then and now. To scan that context systemically means that we must enquire about its vision, its structures, its means and methods. But first we should mention certain general characteristics of systems.

Because the parts of a system are inter-related, if real change is to take place, all of it will have to change. Unless the total system changes, nothing will really change. Minor modifications may take place, 'changes' may happen but they will be quickly neutralised by the *homeostasis* of the system. Furthermore, because it is a stratified system, one may contribute to oppression in it not only through unjust decisions but also (and above all) by merely maintaining one's position or attempting to 'better' it. Another characteristic of systems is that people generally behave within them as if there were no alternative. So at the time of Jesus, the strong and the weak, the rich and poor, the Pharisee and publican were investing their energy in maintaining the stability of an apparently irreformable, divinely sanctioned system.

Since Jesus was concerned with an alternative, he would have to propose a way of releasing the human energy that had become congealed into the maintenance of structures and institutions, a way that would speak to the atrophying parts of all his hearers. He would need to be able to liberate some people from false security and others from profound fatalism. This he did by offering a new vision, by introducing a radical restructuring and by employing very different means and methods.

The vision and the foundation of the new structures
Over against the vision which underpinned the prevailing religious system, whose claim to be the covenant community was
belied by its treatment of the poor, he proclaimed the king-
dom/reign of God as known to him. The choice facing his hearers
then was: Abba or Mammona. Did they acknowledge the gracious and prodigal power at the heart of human life and seek to
embody that generous impulse by nurturing all life? Or did they
distort that power by parleying it into self-serving schemes that
destroyed others and ultimately the self.

To those who prided themselves on being candidates for the
kingdom because of their moral, religious or spiritual achievements, he announced that the kingdom belonged to the poor
whom they despised as godless sinners. In contrast to the daunt-
ing criteria for entry into the kingdom proposed by the powerful
within the holiness system, he declared that the reign of God
was most intensively active among the poor because they were
poor. This partiality prevailed, not because of the inner dispositions of the poor and not because of the 'value' of poverty (it is
an anti-value), but because God is the God who abhors the dehumanising oppression to which the poor were being subjected.
As the God of life whose 'will it is that none of his children perish', where else would God be found except where humanity
and life itself was most threatened, as it was among the poor.
God is active there to overcome that numbing, inhuman situation and to 'bless the poor', and so it is through their cry that
God speaks infallibly.

Jesus however did not 'curse' the wealthy. Rather he said, 'Woe
to you that are wealthy for you have received your consolation.'
(Luke 6:24) The 'wealthy' were to grieve because they were
wealthy, and not because they were singularly evil according to
moral or religious criteria. Their situation is grievous because
their wealth denies access to the Abba of the poor. If the reign of
God were to touch their lives they must abjure Mammon and re-
linquish their pursuit of possessions, power and prestige and join
with Jesus and the poor in creating a new way of being together.

Nothing could be more shocking or scandalous (Mark 11:6) than
this preaching. Nothing could be more subversive of the sectarian
religious structures which were turned upside down and inside
out. The change proposed was total. It went to the root of all op-

pression. Guided by the cry of the poor and oppressed, Jesus sought to establish new 'relations of grace'[3] and structures which would ensure that none of the iniquities of the old system would ever again be found among the children of the one Abba.

Jesus does not speak about this kingdom/reign of God or dream about alternative structures – he enacts it. To do this he has only his own bodily presence as medium of communication (and that of his disciples) to incarnate its presence and make its power concrete and palpable. Some of the choices he makes – giving up his trade, becoming an intinerant preacher, being homeless, speak of the consistency of that enactment. It is only from a position of freely chosen solidarity with the poor and those classified as sinners that he can credibly proclaim the all-inclusive love of God. Proclamation from any other position would still be at the expense of the poor, even if it claimed to speak in their name. The gospels describe his many interventions to deliver the poor, the oppressed, the suffering from their real misery. His humane praxis of the kingdom is carried out in solidarity with the outcasts of society, in service to the despised, the broken, the lost. He restores their humanity to them, reintegrates them into the community, brings them God's forgiveness and shalom. In response to him, these people experience a new lease of life, feel a new future opening up for them, are drawn to struggle for a new way of being human together. In this way he reverses the multiple excommunications of the holiness system and reintegrates those excluded, even the dead.

Bread
Because he is concerned with proclaiming and celebrating life and humanity in the name of God, he must be a ritualist. He must engage with what human beings can do with configurations of fire, air, earth and water. Bread, a product of these elements, 'fruit of the earth and work of human hands', in that culture was the indispensable food, the symbol of life itself and of the overcoming of death. But that elemental symbol evoked many narratives and rituals. It recalled the theological stories of God's creation and ongoing providence and the 'good earth' and the gift of 'the land' and even the 'bread of affliction'. To have bread raised ethical questions – about how it was obtained, who might have been deprived of it and the imperative to share it. (Is 58:7, Ez 18:7) It also raised social and cultural and communitarian

questions, for com-panionship literally means bread-sharing. Finally, it raised eschatological questions, for 'eating bread together in the kingdom' (Is 25:6-8) had become a symbol of the Messianic age. (See Lk 14:15)

Bread-breaking

Bread-breaking[4] was not peculiar to Jews for it is the great universal ritual, but for Jews to take bread was always to take what was already given, and so their first response must be a blessing-prayer, a *berakah*. The bread has then been removed from an indifferent condition and has been referred to the mystery of God. In turn, those at table are understood to share in God's blessing which brings peace, brotherhood, sisterhood and forgiveness. Then the bread was broken so that what was necessary for sustaining one's own life was given away for the other. It thus unites all those who share in this single source of life. To do this ritually with what sustains life implies the possibility of giving away even life itself for someone, someday, should it be demanded. The meal ritual then is grace, with all its rich register of meanings, made palpable.

Jesus, the Jew, also engaged in bread-breaking, but the content and meaning of even that ritual are changed radically when we note the context and company in which it took place. It became his most consummate enactment of the kingdom. Those who regarded themselves as righteous before God broke bread only with other like-minded people, in the conviction that thereby they enjoyed communion with God and with each other. By contrast, Jesus' bread-breaking was indiscriminate, unconditional, all-inclusive. He seated Zealots and publicans, pharisees and prostitutes, wealthy and poor, 'tax collectors and sinners' together at table and so cut through the distinctions, stratifications and taboos that surrounded that ritual, in a scandalous way. For this he was called a 'glutton and a drunkard.' (Lk 7:34) His behaviour raised the disturbing questions: 'Why does the master eat with tax-collectors and sinners?' (Mt 2:16), 'Why does the master serve at table? (Lk 12:37). Just as his story about the man on the road to Jericho enabled his hearers to join together the words 'Samaritan' and 'neighbour', which had been kept apart for six hundred years, so his ritual at table broke down the dividing wall maintained between tables for centuries. Through that ritual he opened up communion with other women and

men and access to God as Abba, so he became the ingatherer and
the living covenant. We notice too how in the gospel accounts of
the multiplication of the loaves (see Mk 6 – feeding 5,000 Jews;
Mk 8 – feeding 4,000 Gentiles; Jn 6), Jesus *took* loaves that had already been given as a gift, *blessed* God in thankfulness and *broke*
them and *gave* them away. Here the universal implications of
bread-breaking and ingathering are being communicated.

Enda McDonagh has reminded us[5] that we live in a self–consuming universe, and deep within us is the tension between the
need to consume and to commune. It is possible to scan the
ministry of Jesus as a struggle to overcome the ravages of consumption and to establish communion. His action at table is the
paradigm of this new human way of being together, where consumption is determined by the needs of the other and where
communion is established in and through controlled consumption.

In Mark 2, we see that discipleship is linked to table-fellowship.
What happens ritually, and therefore really, at table must become a permanent way of life. Jesus invites disciples to respond
to the kingdom by being together in such a way as to make credible the dream that God has for the world. He asks them to live
in service to the humanity of others, so that the roots of oppression, the pathologies of the heart – the hunger for power, prestige and possessions – would be overcome.

But those who wanted to grasp, and hoard and cling to the old
ways and the old securities were deeply threatened by Jesus'
humane praxis of the kingdom and attitudes hardened and opposition to him deepened. His ministry could have been perceived
as a threat to the role of the Temple, the interests of the
Sadducees and the security of the Roman occupying forces. It
seemed expedient that he should die.

Facing death

If we are to understand why Jesus faces death, we need to
appreciate the systemic as well as the personal and theological
significance of what he said and did. All that we have seen of his
ministry of solidarity with the dehumanised, threatened the religious, political and ecomonic system, for it proposed a radical
and dangerous alternative. The new way of being human together
which he lived, demanded a life of service to all. The leader of

such a grouping should be 'slave to all'. (Mk 10:44) Such a revisionist understanding of authority was repugnant to both the Jewish and Roman leadership who, despite external differences, shared exactly the same mentality. They understood only how to destroy humanity; Jesus sought to liberate and nurture human being. Together the leaders colluded to destroy Jesus. Although these hostile forces threaten to consume him, he will not abandon his mission nor meet violence with violence. Only the way of hopeful and transforming acceptance of the future, even if it should involve suffering and death, remains. In fidelity to Abba and in solidarity with the poor and the outcast, he undertakes the final journey to Jerusalem. Luke tells us that on the way he continues to cherish and gather to himself the poor, the sick, the feeble, the broken-hearted and the lost. Was it his final undoing that he dared to bring such a group of 'unholy' people into the Holy City?

Given the significance of meals in his ministry, it is not surprising that when Jesus was face to face with death he should draw on the appropriate and powerful symbolism of the table-ritual to communicate the deepest meaning of his life and oncoming death.

Last Supper narratives
When we turn to the New Testament narratives of that Last Supper we are immediately confronted by the diversity and complexity of these texts. The Synoptics (Lk 22:19-20, Mk 14:22-24, Mt 26:26-28) give their respective communities an account of the words and actions of Jesus at table, set within their distinctive Last Supper narratives, which are in turn set within their Passion narratives. Paul's account (1 Cor 11:23 ff), whose origins can be traced back to the late 30s, offers a recollection and application of the institution of the 'Lord's Supper' to the divided church at Corinth. Through these texts we are alerted to the pluralism of eucharistic thought, interpretation and practice, within a common framework, which existed in the early communities.

Faced with this diversity and pluralism, some scholars have pursued the way of historical reconstruction of the Last Supper. But substantial disagreement still exists among them concerning what Jesus actually did and said, the day of the Supper, its Paschal character, the dates of the various traditions etc.

Other scholars prefer to treat the texts as narratives which have come down to us as part of a living, ecclesial tradition. As such they reflect the eucharist faith of the early communities, which must be taken as the reliable basis for understanding the eucharist. Further insight into these narratives, they suggest, may be gained by taking account of what we know of the common life of these communities. From texts such as Acts 2:42ff and 1 Cor 10-11, we recognise that our understanding of the significance of the sharing of the eucharistic bread and cup within these communities must be related to the wider sharing of life and resources which took place there. That sharing is founded on their unity in the Word that brought them to birth and which is discovered anew in their table-sharing, and finds powerful expression in common ownership of assets, in common meals, in mutual care and service and in their struggle with social stratification.

Cultic and testamentary tradition

Xavier Leon-Dufour,[6] referring to the narratives of the last meal of Jesus, distinguishes between the testamentary tradition and the cultic tradition. Precedents for the testamentary tradition are found in the First Testament and in Apocryphal literature, where certain individuals, knowing that death is imminent, gather their relatives and friends and in a farewell discourse, review their lives, addresses the future and exhort their hearers to live uprightly. He sees the exemplary washing of the feet, the final meal and the farewell discourse in John (13-17) as belonging to that genre. By contrast, the accounts in the Synoptics and Paul are seen to reflect the cultic tradition and provide an authoritative foundation for the church's eucharistic ritual. Yet he believes that elements of the testamentary may be found in the cultic tradition. Jesus' teaching about service ('I am among you as one who serves') and leadership ('The leader as one who serves') in Luke 22:24-38 after the sharing of the cup, could be part of such a tradition. So too the 'detached' references to "he fruit of the vine' (Mt 26-29, Mk 14:25, Lk 22:19) may indicate that the synoptic accounts of Jesus' interpretation of the bread and cup were part of a longer farewell discourse.

The washing of the feet must be seen as a powerful symbolic interpretation by Jesus of his life and ministry of service which parallels and complements the interpretation offered through the gift of bread and wine in the cultic tradition. Jesus' ministry of service to the humanity of those dehumanised by the religious and political systems has brought him to this hour. He continues it, even at table, and offers it as his last testament and final exhortation to his disciples. The testamentary tradition then serves as a salutary reminder that Jesus Christ wishes to be united to disciples, not only in the eucharistic celebrations but through imitation of his loving service to the outcast and the lost. Both modes of presence are indispensable.

The setting

Before turning to the table narratives themselves, we should pay attention to the setting of the meal. The Synoptics see it as part of the Passion narrative and Paul reminds us that it took place 'on the night that he was betrayed' (11:23 b), so in all the sources it is very closely linked to his suffering and death. Paul regards Passover as a key to understanding the death of Christ (1 Cor 5:7), yet he never links it to the Supper. For John, the last meal of Jesus could not have been a Passover Seder, but the Synoptics are emphatic that it was. Given this vexed impasse, many exegetes agree that while we cannot be certain that it was a Passover meal, we must admit that it took place at Passover time and are justified in speaking of the meal being eaten within a Passover 'atmosphere'. That festive week would have been replete with vibrant memories and hopes of salvation, and the 'poem of the Four Nights' (A Targum on Exodus 12:42 dating from the end of the first century) which recalls the great deeds of God in the history of Israel and expresses longing for the coming of Messiah, may put us in touch with that atmosphere. It celebrates the pivotal Passover nights of Israel's history – the night of creation, of the sacrifice of Isaac, of the liberation from Egypt and the longed-for night of Passover when Messiah will come. Yet we must remember that, finally, the actions and prayers of Passover cannot help us to understand Jesus' unique actions and words of institution in themselves. Within Passover, the bread and wine rituals could never have had the meaning he gives them here. What is to be remembered and celebrated is now identified, not with the events of Israel's history, but with the history and destiny of Jesus.

The immediate setting for the last meal of Jesus according to the Synoptics is marked by intense expectation (Lk 22:15 ff) and awesome finality. In all the accounts we have a saying of Jesus, which is almost universally accepted as authentic, in which he declares that he will 'not drink again of the fruit of the vine until that day when I drink it new in the kingdom of God' (Mk 14:25); Mt 26:29 adds 'with you in my father's kingdom'; Lk 22:18 has 'until the kingdom of God comes'). In Jesus' vision this is literally the last cup of earthly fellowship before the final realisation of God's kingdom. We must remember too how references to betrayal, denial, infidelity, failure, lack of solidarity and misunderstanding, are interwoven in these narratives.

Similarities and differences

When dealing with the cultic accounts of Jesus' actions and words – the institution narratives – it is usual to pair Paul and Luke (PL) and Mark and Matthew (M). When we read a parallel version of these texts, both the similarities and differences between the two sets become obvious. PL tell us that Jesus took the cup 'after the supper' so the blessing prayers and the words of interpretation over the bread and the cup are separated by a meal; M gives no indication of any such separation. The command 'Do this in memory of me' is found only in PL (twice in Paul). PL have the phrase 'for you' over the bread (and cup in Luke) whereas M has the phrase 'for many' over the cup. Finally we notice that the parallelism body/covenant in PL becomes the more symmetrical body/blood in M.

Commentators also frequently contrast the theological resonances found in both sets of texts. They point to the prophetic theology, reflected in PL, that was critical of the formalism of Israel's worship and looked to the establishment of a new covenant. (Jer 31:31-34, Ez 36:26-28) M recalls the covenant-sacrifice of Exodus (Ex 24:3-8) and the cultic-sacrificial preoccupations of the Pentateuch. Yet these theological strains should not be opposed, for they are bound together in the narratives by the theology of the suffering servant.

The actions

The discrepancies between the versions of the words of Jesus in PL and M have led scholars to begin their analysis with the relatively uniform accounts of the actions of Jesus. In dramatic terms Jesus is the chief actor, but the disciples too are active though we are offered no description of their actions. We must acknowledge too the presence of the 'multitude' and of God, who though not named explicitly, is present and active. We must keep the dialogical character of the entire narratives in mind all the time.

Jesus' actions at table are described in detail, which is unusual because most of them (taking, blessing, giving) were simply the gestures of table-fellowship whose meaning we have seen. (But as so often happens with ritual, a new symbolic depth may be discovered within it while the externals remain the same, and it is only the interpretative word that alerts us to this newness). However, it is reported that at table, Jesus broke with traditional ritual in an unprecedented way by passing a *single* cup to all the disciples and also by adding future-directed words of interpretation to the sharing of the broken bread. Some commentators appeal to the symbolic actions of the prophets (especially Jeremiah 19, 27, 28, and Ezekiel 4:1-3, 5:1-4, 12:1ff), to shed light on these actions of Jesus (and indeed all his actions). Such prophetic enactments were the anticipatory realisation in symbol of some future event. Accordingly they see Jesus, the eschatological prophet, anticipating in symbolic action his definitive self-giving and the new life that will come from it. While such a comparison may be helpful, we must remember that unlike the usual prophetic actions Jesus' actions and words require the collaborative responses of eating and drinking from the disciples. Finally, all four accounts tell us that after taking the bread Jesus pronounced a blessing prayer or gave thanks, which are themselves actions in the proper sense. We have no account of the form these blessing prayers took.

The words over the bread

In attending to the words over the bread, we will follow PL and cross refer to M. These words communicate the meaning and significance the life, death and destiny of Jesus of Nazareth in symbolic compression. The richness of reference refracted through them means that their interpretation can never be easy, and our own presuppositions about them compound that difficulty. In particular, inherited misunderstandings which equate sacrifice with death and inadequate models of salvation, may need to be resisted. We may need to remind ourselves that the constant stress here is on life. All four accounts attribute the words 'This is my body' to Jesus. 'Body' in biblical anthropology is not something human beings *have*, they *are* bodies. 'Body' is not just what is contained within the skin; it refers to the person as expressing and manifesting the entire, living self. It is the medium of communication, that which is at the centre of a web of relationships and relatedness. Yet to speak of the person as 'body' also implies human vulnerability and their nature as beings-for-death.

Luke's version of the words which qualify 'body' are 'which (is) given for you'; Paul's is 'which (is) for you'. This means that Jesus is willing to give his very life, even to the point of death. He is willing to forego the life that he now lives, the communication and communion already established, for the sake of new life, a deeper communion, a more profound communication, a radically new form of presence. He has succeeded in integrating even the prospect of death into his mission, in the conviction that God's designs cannot be gainsaid but will emerge in sovereign freedom. By giving this blessed, life-giving bread as his body to the disciples, he is stressing life rather than death. Even with his 'body given' comes the promise of renewed fellowship that is stronger than death. Those to whom the broken bread is 'given' (M and Luke) are to be the foundation members of the new community gathered by his presence and breaking bread in his memory.

In memory

Luke and Paul (2) have the command: 'Do this in memory (or to make remembrance) of me'. The word in Greek here is *anamnesis*, but behind it is the biblical concept of *zikkaron* which was mentioned at the end of the last chapter. Against the people's amnesia, their forgetfulness of their relationship to God and to each other, the bible issues repeated calls to 'remember'. They are to make remembrance by celebrating in story and ritual God's mighty deeds on their behalf in ongoing creation and history. This is no mere subjective recall on their behalf nor it is an attempt to repeat events that are historically past. Rather it is undertaken out of the conviction that, through the power of the God who is intimate to all time, their ritual will be suffused by the meaning and significance of the reality they are celebrating. Their *zikkaron* ritual will become, as it were, a medium through which the God of the covenant can act to transform mind and imagination and heart. They in turn will once again be inspired and empowered to act in ways consistent with their identity as God's elected people and in harmony with the meaning of God's salvific deeds which are remembered. The Passover celebration is the paradigm of all of this.

This command formula in PL recalls, structurally, the ordinance to keep Passover: 'This day is to be a day of remembrance (*le zikkaron*) for you, and you must celebrate it as a feast in Yahweh's honour. (Ex 12:14) And indeed there are many parallels between the celebration of Passover and what is taking place at table.[7] However, they are commanded by Jesus to make remembrance, not of events in the history of the nation, but startlingly 'of me'. What is to be remembered and celebrated now is identified with the person of Jesus. They are to make remembrance by doing 'this', that is the specific actions involving the bread and cup, but those actions, as we have noted, never have *that* meaning for Israelites then or now. Jesus has decentred the meaning of the religious meals (even Passover) which lay at the heart of Israel's life and worship and with sovereign authority replaced it by himself.

We must note too the parallel between 'me' and 'my body', 'my blood'. His whole ministry, his preaching and enacting of the kingdom of God, are recapitulated in these potent gestures and interpretative words at table. But the core direction of the past, present and future of his love is also gathered therein, as is his loving fidelity to Abba's kingdom, his commitment to solidarity with victims even to the point of death, and his conviction that God's love is stronger than the dark mystery of death that looms before him. Through his 'given body' and blood 'shed' the God of salvation will *somehow* but *certainly* ingather the multitude. This is the new unsurpassable deed of God. The new life, which is to be achieved through this giving over of himself, will be available to his disciples and the multitude. But, lest they forget its source, they are to make remembrance of him as he has commanded and in that way they will be empowered to serve each other in justice and love. Here we see again the link between the emphases of the cultic and the testamentary tradition, and acknowledge the similarities between the command in PL and Jesus' words 'I have given you example that you may copy what I have done to you'. (Jn 13:15)

The words over the cup

Luke and Paul tell us that Jesus took the cup 'after the Supper' saying: 'This cup is the new covenant in my blood'. This cup is the one cup that Jesus, in a totally unprecedented action, offers to all his disciples so it signifies communion and intimacy. Like the covenant which it symbolises, it remains one even as it is shared. In the biblical tradition, 'cup' could be symbolic of the will of God or connote extreme tribulation (Lk 22:42) or denote the cup of salvation or the joyful cup that brims over. Perhaps all of these meanings are verified here.

The 'new covenant' obviously recalls the prophecies of the prophets Jeremiah (31:31-34) and Ezekiel (36:26-28), but the metaphor itself is multivalent and so includes reference to the covenant with Abraham, the mosaic covenant and, most importantly, the suffering servant who is 'given as a covenant to the people'. (42:6, 49:8) Jeremiah and Ezekiel spoke of a new covenant to be established through God's initiative. Isaiah saw the figure of the servant as the necessary mediator between God and Israel through whose fidelity and commitment unto death God establishes the covenant. Although Isaiah does not describe this covenant as 'new', its unprecedented character invites such a description.

Throughout his ministry, Jesus had opened up access to God and graciously held open God's future to those deprived of it. This communion with God and others, which he had achieved through the mediation of his own bodily presence, his self as body and blood, is the very purpose of covenant in Israel. Now according to PL that living, 'informal' covenant is to become definitively ratified 'in the blood' of Jesus. The inauguration of covenant is always God's initiative so it can never be a result of human achievement or even virtue. So 'covenant in my blood' suggests that the fidelity of Jesus unto death will be the means by which God's sovereign *hesed* will establish a new covenant relationship with the disciples (L) and with all human beings (M). The new covenant, which is being inaugurated by God through Jesus' destiny, fulfils and far surpasses the dreams of Jeremiah, Ezekiel and even Isaiah.

'Blood' in the bible does not simply refer to what courses through the veins and arteries. It stands for the 'person' as living, animate, with emphasis on the life-principle which is at the disposal of God alone. To speak of his blood as 'shed' (as Luke and M do) indicates that he is pouring out his very soul on behalf of the disciples and the multitude. It intimates that the death will be premature and violent, but again because the 'new covenant' is offered as drink that comforts and cheers, it is the sharing of new enhanced *life* deriving from it that is being stressed.

In Mark and Matthew's version Jesus says: 'This is my blood of the covenant which is shed for the multitude', so, as in Luke, 'my blood which is shed' is indissolubly linked to 'covenant'. The phrase, 'This is my blood of the covenant' recalls Moses' proclamation, 'Behold the blood of the covenant which the Lord has made with you' (Ex 24:8), accompanying his unique action of sprinkling the altar and the people with blood from a communion sacrifice. Exodus had involved liberation from slavery and the gathering of these liberated slaves (marked off by blood) (Ex 12:23-38) into a new egalitarian unity. The covenant established a new blood-relationship between these liberated slaves and the God who had liberated them. Yet the differences and contrasts between the two statements are overwhelming: the blood of animals/'my blood'; a cup of blood sprinkled externally/personally drinking the cup of the covenant; the exodus from slavery and the covenant with Israel/the new Exodus into a new freedom which will overcome even death itself and a new covenant between God as Ababa and *all* people. So while M does not refer to it as 'new', the newness of this covenant, epitomised by 'in my blood', is obvious.

'Communion sacrifice' or 'peace offerings', as the names suggest, were concerned with union and communion between the offerer and God (which indeed is the purpose of all sacrifice). They included proclamatory praise and a joyful meal with friends and neighbours in the presence of God, at which part of the slaughtered animal was eaten. While M's version of the words recall the communion sacrifice at Sinai (Ex 24:11), we must again acknowledge the uniqueness of what is being said and done at the table. The recall of the language of cultic ritual does indeed link Jesus' actions and words to all that has gone before, but it may bring with it the temptation to try to contain them within those institutions, if the metaphorical nature of its predication is forgotten.[8]

In M's version, the blood is 'shed for the multitude' (Luke has 'for you'). This phrase recalls the fate of the servant who was dedicated to thankless service and was willing to endure all manner of grievous suffering and contempt, 'who poured out his soul to death … while bearing the faults of the multitude'. (Is 53:12) Yet, as noted above, through his fidelity and freely-endured suffering, he becomes a mediator between God and those who have caused him to suffer. Jesus is declaring that his own imminent suffering will be used by God to establish a new, gracious dispensation, surpassing all others, in which all women and men will share.

Matthew adds the words 'for the forgiveness of sins', which again are reminiscent of the servant who is described as 'bearing the sin of the multitude' (53:12) and whose voluntary suffering is seen as 'an offering for sin'. (53:10) It reminds us that forgiveness of sin is a condition for and a fruit of the covenant.

Easter

Jesus goes forth from the supper room to the garden of agony, where the convictions of the table seem to be temporarily undone. Then follows his final betrayal and arrest. Pilate releases Barabbas and sends the other son of Abba away to be crucified. But Abba, whose love sustains him in life, loves him into fullness of life, which we call resurrection. The crucified-risen Jesus, who has taken humanity into the heart of God, is thereby at the heart of humanity.

His new presence to disciples convinces them that, in life and glory, he offers grace and salvation and new life, and that offer cannot be rescinded by any force or power, not even by death. After Easter, that offer was experienced above all as gracious forgiveness and reconciliation after their abandonment of him. It re-establishes discipleship by bringing it to a new level of intimacy. It is no wonder then that forgiveness and Easter are inextricably linked (Lk 24:47, Jn 20:22-23, Acts 5:31, 10:43, 26:23, I Cor 15:17-18) and that disciples are said to exercise a 'ministry of reconciliation'. (2 Cor 5:18)

We notice too how frequently the theme of ingathering occurs (Lk 24:33, Jn 19:20, 26, Acts 1:6, 2:1) and this ingathering reaches out to the ends of the earth. (Acts 1:8, Mt 28:19) This is no mere assembly of individuals but they are described as 'being of one mind and heart'. (Acts 1:8, Mt 28:19) This is no mere assembly of individuals but they are described as 'being of one mind and heart'. (Acts 1:14-15, 2:1, 44, 47) Again the taking, blessing and breaking of meal-fellowship is the privileged *locus* for recognising the presence of the Lord (Lk 24:30, Jn 21:13) and disciples are described as 'those who ate and drank with him after his resurrection from the dead'. (Acts 10:41) The joy of sharing in the eucharist and in their common meals, which is an anticipation of the joy of the messianic banquet, is emphasised in Acts 2:46. (See Luke 24) Without this celebration they would forget who they were and what they were called to be. Yet we know they did forget and, as the Last Supper narratives forewarned us, failure and sin could be found even at the eucharistic table. Paul tackles this problem in his letter to the Corinthians.

The Corinthian problem

The communal meal, celebrated among people of the same social strata, was a powerful integrating force at all levels of society at Corinth. In the process of evangelisation, the existence of the communal meal was surely an important asset in forming a bridge between the Corinthian culture and Christianity, with its common meals and celebrations of the Lord's Supper. Yet an ambivalence remained, for Christian table-fellowship sought to overcome the very stratifications and distinctions which were expressed and consolidated through the communal meals of Corinthian culture. In that particular setting, the temptation for converts to go back over the bridge and re-establish contact with their pre-Christian roots must have been strong. Paul believed that this was happening, that instead of being conformed to Christ they were reforming him in their own image and likeness. The eucharistic celebration of the Christ cult was being evacuated of its real content and was being replaced by what was acceptable at the cultural level.

The questions raised in chapters 10 and 11 of the First Letter to the Corinthians have to do with the significance of rituals of eating and drinking. Paul declared that eating food which had come from pagan sacrifices did not compromise the faith of Christians, unless there was question of scandalising vulnerable consciencs. By contrast, he was utterly opposed to Christians participating in pagan cultic meals because he believed that it put them in touch with demonic forces. The eucharistic 'blessing cup' and 'the bread which we break' establish the closest possi-

ble personal communion between participants and Christ (16),
and 'because there is one bread, we who are many (the multitude) are one body, for we all partake of the one bread' (17). So
'you cannot partake of the table of the Lord and the table of
demons'. (21) We must note the ease with which Paul's thought
moves from 'the body of Christ' to the multitude who are a single body. It seems that 'the body of Christ' for Paul refers both to
what Jesus of Nazareth has become through death and resurrection, and to what Christians are becoming through him. 'For by
one spirit we are all baptised into one body – Jews and Greeks,
slaves and free – and all are made to drink of the one spirit'.
(12:13, see Gal 3:27-28) The old 'I' is now part of the new 'we',
the one body of the Lord, and this unity should be most dramatically evident when ritually they become partakers of the one
bread and the one cup. But this is not the case, as we see from
chapter 11. Interestingly, what alerts Paul to the inauthenticity
of their celebration of the 'Lord's Supper', is the way in which
the poor are treated.

Chapter 11 contains many images of gathering (17, 18, 20, 33, 34)
but there are also ominous references to scattering, factions and
divisions. Furthermore, there is the painful contrast between the
'Lord's Supper' and the privatised 'meal' of some participants. It
is difficult to reconstruct the details behind these tensions, but it
seems that when they 'assembled as a church' the wealthy mon-
opolised the best food and drink and places. Poorer Christians,
including slaves, who arrived after the meal had begun, had
only their own modest fare or the 'left overs' of the wealthy –
'one is hungry and another is drunk' (21), 'you humiliate those
who have nothing' (22). These Christians are saying one thing
ritually, namely that they are doing what Jesus Christ did, so
that by sharing one bread they may be one body, but doing another – embarrassing those who are poor and eating and drinking too much. In a word, while declaring that they are eating the
Lord's Supper, their real haste is to eat their own without wait-
ing for the others to arrive. (1 Cor 11:21) This group is so divided
that they are dividing Christ. They are attempting to participate
in the eucharistic body of Christ by eating and drinking at the
table, while ignoring the body of Christ around the table. If nothing substantial has changed in their sensitivity to the poor, they
are not 'discerning the body'.(29) To attempt to celebrate the
Lord's Supper despite such disunity, means for Paul that they are

involved in an activity which is so utterly self-contradictory, so false, that they are lying in the most profound way possible. They are using sacred ritual to lie to God and each other about God and each other. It is not that nothing happens, for Paul is emphatic about the unambiguous realism of Christ's presence, rather what happens makes them 'guilty of profaning the body and blood of the Lord'.(27)

In response to this intolerable travesty of the eucharist, Paul seeks to realign their action at table with commitment to service, by reminding them of what 'the Lord Jesus did on the night that he was betrayed'. He wishes to remind the forgetful Corinthians that they gather in response to the Lord's own invitation, that he is present and presides at this table of anamnesis. So they must gather as 'one body' and behave accordingly when they have gathered, or else they 'eat and drink their own condemnation.'(29) Furthermore, their repetition of the Lord's own interpretation of his life and death in this divisive situation would stand in judgement on the Corinthians' practical misinterpretation of it. The consistency between what Jesus did at table and in the whole of his life, demands consistency between what happens at the eucharistic table and what happens at other tables, and indeed in the whole of life.

By way of powerful and challenging summary of what he has sought to communicate, Paul declares, 'Each time you eat this bread and drink this cup, you proclaim the death of the Lord until he comes'.(26) It is almost as if Paul is trying to shock the Corinthians into a realisation of the seriousness of what they are doing. Yet it must not be misunderstood as some kind of morbid preoccupation with the crucifixion. It is the death of the Lord that is being proclaimed, that is the new life, grace and salvation that have come through the death and resurrection of the Lord. And this proclamation takes place because they are gathered by his life-giving power, in his anamnesis. When they break the bread and share the cup in his name that proclamation of salvation in him is most powerfully articulated so that it may be internalised in a transforming way.

In his ministry, Jesus of Nazareth sought to gather women and men into an new unity where sin, in all its complex forms, would be overcome, and none of the oppressiveness of the old ways could prevail. As the Lord Jesus, through whose death the new and eternal covenant has been established, he continues that ministry in a universal way. How then can Christians gather around the Lord's table while despising or merely ignoring the poor and the needy? How can they come together in the name of this new covenant of unity without a minimum of unity among themselves? How can they proclaim and celebrate the new life that comes from the Lord Jesus and continue to diminish the life of those he loves preferentially? These questions are as relevant for us today as they were for the Corinthians then.

Notes

1. Mc Cabe, H., *God Matters*, Chapman, 1987, chapter 8.

2. Tamez, Elsa, *Bible of the Oppressed*, Orbis, 1982.

3. Mackey, J. P., *Modern Theology*, Oxford University Press, 1987, 93-94, 114-116.

4. ibid, 104-112.

5. N. D. S. W., Gill and Macmillan, 1990, p 750.

6. *Sharing the Eucharistic Bread*, Paulist Press, 1987, pp 82-95.

7. ibid, p 111.

8. *Disturbing the Peace*, pp 247-250.

Epilogue

That reflection on the problems of the Corinthian church is an appropriate ending for this book. Paul's salutary reminder about the need for commitment and consistency in our discipleship needs to be heard every day. We need to be reminded that being called in the Spirit around the communion table of the Lord, means that we must be actively concerned about those who may be excluded, or only inadequately included, in our assemblies. To be guests at the table where the Lord is host means being commissioned to struggle along with the poor and the oppressed, to endeavour to include the excluded and the marginalised. It means being aware of the power of the language we use in the anamnesis of the Lord, and its role in shaping our lives, and yet acknowledging the tension between language and action.

To 'proclaim the death of the Lord' means including, as lamentation, the unseparable sufferings of our world. To take what is 'fruit of the earth and work of human hands' is to recall the travail of creation itself and our bewildered complicity in the destruction of the 'good Earth'. Yet this is a hope-full remembering, for it is joined to the anamnesis of Christ. Through that anamnesis we are given a fragmentary glimpse of what a world transformed in his likeness could be like, and we are impelled to struggle with him for its fulfilment in our praxis and praise.